MW00398003

Expectant

40 Devotions for New and Expectant Moms

Julie Sanders

This publication is a creative work protected in full by all applicable copyright laws, as well as by misappropriation, trade secret, unfair competition, and other applicable laws. No part of this book may be reproduced or transmitted in any manner without written permission from Hallway Publishing, except in the case of brief quotations embodied in critical articles or reviews. All rights reserved.

Hallway Publishing
2701 Del Paso Road, 130-92
Sacramento, CA 95835

hallwaypublishing.com
Contact Information: info@thehallwayproject.com

Expectant

COPYRIGHT © 2014 by Julie Sanders
First Edition, November 2014

Cover Art by Winter Goose Publishing
Typeset by Odyssey Books

ISBN: 978-1-941058-20-6

Published in the United States of America

Scripture Notice

All Scripture quotations are taken from the *Holy Bible, English Standard Version*, copyright 2001 by Crossway Bibles, a division of Good News Publishers. Used by permission. All rights reserved.

To the crowd of young women around me, near and far, who entered motherhood in a variety of ways during the last two years.
With names like Shea, Jodi, Sara, Kayla, Gabi, Ana, Jessica, Sarah, Kellie, Jill, Brooks, Kyra,
Ashley, Lindsey, Renee, Rebecca, and more, they inspired me to write from my heart
to theirs when they began their journeys of expectation.
It has been a joy to watch you grow in every way.
You are beautiful new moms.

Most of all, to my own first baby, JoHanna, now grown.
Being her mother has been better than I expected and more than I dreamed.
You have truly been "God's gracious gift" to us, and I hope your heart will always be
EXPECTANT for what He has for you.

Contents

 # Introduction

Dear sweet new mom or mom-to-be,

If you are reading this book, then you must have an expectant heart. You either long to be on the journey of motherhood, or you've already begun. Because I know first-hand how great a joy comes with becoming a mommy, I want to encourage those of you who are just starting out. From one mother's heart to another, I want you to know God has a tender heart for mothers and will be with us every baby-step of the way. To understand why I already love you and am praying for you as you become a mom, I want to share a little bit of how I understand the pleasure and the pain of an expectant heart.

The night we decided to try for a baby, we ate cheeseburgers and smiled more widely than the sesame-seed buns on our plates. Thinking it was the right time in so many ways, we agreed to take the parenting plunge. We had no idea what awaited.

While I carried our child, I also carried ideas and hopes and assumptions about how my arrival into motherhood would unfold. Following all of the doctor's orders, planning for the baby's arrival, and listening to a chorus of well-meaning wisdom, we had no reason to think our expectations were unrealistic.

We signed up for birthing classes like all good parents-to-be, but I decided I didn't need to stay for the session covering emergency deliveries and C-sections. After all, we expected a smooth end to my pregnancy. I anticipated working as a first-grade teacher right up until my due date, delivering with my doctor, staying briefly in the hospital, recovering quickly while I lost my baby weight, and enjoying our sweet newborn in the first miraculous weeks together.

After marking off the thirty-eighth week on my planner, I went to bed feeling like a mature beluga whale. Before daylight dawned, we knew something wasn't right. Nothing happened like the books said it would or like we planned. We hurried to the hospital on icy roads, where an unpredictable, out of the ordinary story unfolded.

The sleepy doctor broke the news that I was having a placental abruption. He shouted for the new shift of medical staff to hurry to the operating room where my husband put me on the table and held my hand as I lost consciousness. I wasn't aware of the moment they pulled our limp baby from my belly and whisked her off to revive her. Her first delicate days of life were spent across town at a neonatal intensive care unit, while I fought to hold on with little memory of how the pregnancy ended. Hushed visitors came and prayed and went. None of it resembled the images we dreamed about.

It wasn't until I became pregnant, waited thirty-eight weeks, delivered our first-born, and began to mother her, that I realized I had been swollen with my own expectations. The first pages of our baby book looked nothing like what we anticipated; our first fragile months were filled with help from family and friends. We tried to salvage joy from our dashed plans, but I struggled to even recognize myself or feel any bond with the baby I had carried. I grieved the harsh difference between our dreams and our reality.

Eventually, the miracle of new life and the joy of our child overshadowed the hard things and the disappointments. Discovery overcame depression, and healing of body, heart, and mind set in. Painful realities faded into our family history, and we moved on to the wide and welcoming journey of being parents. As our little one grew, so did our ability to look back, be grateful, and sift out the blessings. Today, that little girl baby has grown into a young woman heading off to college with expectations of her own.

Becoming a mother is not an easy task; it rarely unfolds as we think it will, but it also seldom leaves disappointment. No woman knows how her own story will be written, but God's truth provides all you need to meet the challenges of motherhood with wisdom and joy. It's going to be better than you ever imagined, so enter in with a heart that is expectant.

Expectant with you,

Julie

 # YOU

Feeling Your Changes

Expectations

I couldn't believe it. "That's her? That's it? No, really, where's the real one?" I didn't even bother to take a picture.

As the ferry approached Liberty Island, I leaned over the railing to see the magnificent view of the mammoth site I anticipated. Catching my first glimpse of the famous Statue of Liberty, my jaw dropped. From my earliest years, my mind archived images of the iconic symbol, creating a setting, size, and appearance I assumed were all accurate. The moment of arrival left me feeling rather duped and disappointed, wondering how I could've missed the realities of Lady Liberty. It was only in being there that I grasped her true proportions and the position of the world-renowned gift. My expectations were a distant cousin to the truth I discovered.

Before a woman knows it, she begins to tuck images and thoughts about motherhood into her mind and heart. Expectations of how motherhood will look and feel take shape as a doll-toting little girl grows into a pubescent teenager, into a young woman, and then an adult. Interference from fairytales and novels and full-color glossy catalogs makes matters worse. Throw in a baby-bearing friend who puts on a mask of perfection, and an expectant mom may set herself up for a lot of disappointment, guilt, and confusion.

It may not be until she embarks on the journey of childbearing that a woman realizes how unfamiliar her mothering route feels. After months pass in anticipation and she arrives at destination: motherhood, a first-time mommy might wonder at how different reality is from what she envisioned. "No, really, where's the real one?"

A woman's lifetime of expectations prepares her for motherhood, but those expectations don't predict her circumstances. Each parent's journey is unique. Some arrive via the biological route without a heavy struggle. Some pray long and wait. Some experience infertility's challenges. Some dig deep furrows of grief through loss. Some seem to be made for pregnancy, only to face unexpected complications. Some mothers give up their children, only to have them born anew in the hearts of adoptive parents. No journey is the same. Expectations never promise a mother what her way will be.

Each day in motherhood surprises us, so it makes sense the journey there would be the same. Instead of making statements about what will be or what we will have or what will happen, a realistic mom prepares her heart and opens her hands to the way God has for her. He will not be surprised by whatever lies ahead for mother and child, and He will be there for whatever our mom-paths hold.

It was a parent who experienced great grief who declared, "But he knows the way that I take; when he has tried me, I shall come out as gold," (Job 23:10). That's a promise you can expect to have fulfilled, and it's quite a guarantee. After all, Lady Liberty is just copper; I've seen her, and now I know.

Enjoy the journey on the way to motherhood. Open your eyes and take in every detail. Lean over the railing so you don't miss a thing. You really can't imagine what's ahead, but you can be sure it's greater and more amazing than anything you expected.

Words to grow your heart

"Commit your way to the LORD; trust in him,
and he will act." (Psalm 37:5)

Thoughts to treasure in your heart or share with a friend

∞ What has influenced your ideas most about what motherhood will be like? A movie? A book? Another person?
∞ Describe what you think your baby will look and act like. What will you act like as a mom? Your husband as a dad?
∞ What are your expectations of the part God will play in your motherhood?

Fat and Ugly

There are some really cute pregnancy clothes out there. If you time it right and conceive after your girlfriend delivers, you can enjoy her chic hand-me-downs. Some women look forward to prego-wear and, along with the mommy-to-be glow, look great pregnant. Most women reach a place where the mirror is the enemy and "Fat and ugly" is the only honest response to the unending "How do you feel?" questions from people who can't wait to hold your baby.

In my ninth month I felt a definite love/hate connection with the hippos at the zoo. Secretly, I wondered if my body would ever be normal, and I felt guilty that it mattered to me. No one longs to reach hippo proportions, and most don't, but that doesn't mean we don't feel like wallowing in the mud and floating in a river. Can't we be both beautiful and pregnant?

Yes, and we are. From God's perspective and the perspective of our proud mates, the changes in our bodies represent miracles we are all a part of. It's a blessing on our marriages and a promise for our futures, a smile of God in our lives. So why does the *big stage* of the process feel so unlovely?

Other than the fact we may become physically uncomfortable in various real ways, the world around us sets us up to believe *very pregnant* doesn't go with *beautiful*. When models strap on small baby bumps for prego-wear photo shoots, no one makes sure to add padding to their breasts, swelling around their ankles, or width to their hips; the views we're shown are not true. Expectant moms need a big dose of truth.

To grow the maturity it takes to mother another person, we can "no longer be children, tossed to and fro by the waves and carried about by every wind of doctrine, by human cunning, by craftiness in deceitful schemes. Rather, speaking the truth in love, we are to grow up in every way into him who is the head, into Christ," (Ephesians 4:14-15). If we are to resist the cunning marketing and deceit of what beauty really looks like, we have to turn our thoughts expectantly to God's truth. Throw in a few hormones, and we also really appreciate having the truth spoken in love. Like we choose to faithfully take pre-natal vitamins, we have to choose to think on "whatever is true . . ." (Philippians 4:8).

For a time in our pregnancies, we will be big. Our bodies will change. We will physically become someone new. And we will be beautiful.

Words to grow your heart

"Finally, brothers, whatever is true, whatever is honorable, whatever is just, whatever is pure, whatever is lovely, whatever is commendable, if there is any excellence, if there is anything worthy of praise, think about these things." (Philippians 4:8)

Thoughts to treasure in your heart or share with a friend

- ∞ How are you feeling about the physical changes your body is experiencing?
- ∞ Write a statement about the beautiful truth about your body right now.

The Force inside You—Hormones

Our children were little the day we played on the tiny island in the Pacific, small enough to run from side to side and end to end. We soaked in the sunshine and splashed in aquamarine and topaz stripes of water, gathering piles of starfish. With gentle winds on our faces, we could see a change coming in the distance, dark clouds and heavy shadows. While it was still far off, we prepared to brace ourselves for the approaching force, not knowing just what it would mean for us in our happy moment.

Hormones provide the driving force behind a woman's changes. Who knew our bodies were capable of such amazing transformations? To become the studio where the Creator gently shapes and weaves a life, we undergo a total body experience. Enter the power of hormones as contractors to carry out the blue prints of our children, forcing our bodies to bend to the needs of the ones whose lives command the focus of our very blood flow and distribution of our energy. Hormones bring change necessary for a woman to carry and bear life, but they may feel like a storm sweeping over our happy event.

Outward signs in complexion, hair, bodily fluids, digestion, and even fingernails point to the existence of a small person exerting her power. In order to conceive and carry an infant, hormone levels must be optimal, even requiring some moms-to-be and hopeful moms-to-be to take hormone supplements. While chemical levels enable us to carry a child, they may also wreak havoc on our otherwise healthy bodies and our other-wise healthy relationships. A husband may wonder who or what has taken over his wife, turning her into some-one unpredictable and occasionally extreme in her emo-tions. The same woman who wooed him close enough to make their baby might strike fear into his heart as he tries to guess where she is on the hormone coaster. It's a ride an expectant couple cannot get off of for nine months of changes, while the force of hormones dictates the gradual growth of their babe.

So once the nine months pass, can a mom breathe a deep sigh of relief to know the hormone front has passed? After such a long, gradual transformation, a mom should also expect her reversal to take time. The same hormonal storm front that swept in to make way for her baby also requires time to grow calm again. Instead of a momentary event like your water breaking, physical changes in areas like hair, skin, and fluid levels may take weeks or months to return to pre-baby quali-ties, and you might find a *new you* will emerge in some areas. Nursing moms experience a slower release of the baby's control over their bodies, as they produce and release milk in response to their children's needs.

At times, a heavy hormonal blanket covers a new mom physically, emotionally, and mentally in the form of post-partum depression. After all a body goes through to bear a new life, restoring balance to a woman's outlook, energy, and frame of mind may require a labor all its own. Even in the midst of the excitement, fatigue, and changes, a new mom should be honest with a mentor or trusted medical practitioner so she can be the mother her infant needs her to be.

While we huddled together in a beach-side shelter, the storm passed over us. Though we experienced a time of darkness, a strong wind, and a choppy boat ride home, we weathered its force and appreciated the calm that came later.

Hormones must change to carry and bear a baby, but in this season of new things, peace and calm will come again to a new mom's body, mind, and spirit.

Words to grow your heart

"My mouth shall speak wisdom; the meditation of my heart shall be understanding." (Psalm 49:3)
"From the end of the earth I call to You when my heart is faint. Lead me to the rock that is higher than I." (Psalm 61:2)

Thoughts to treasure in your heart or share with a friend

- ∞ What physical changes remind you that you are experiencing hormonal changes?
- ∞ In what ways does your spouse understand the force of your hormones? How could you help him understand?
- ∞ Do you recognize times when you're having a *wave* or even a *tsunami* of hormone related feelings?
- ∞ What can help you manage your changes? Medically? Spiritually? Emotionally? Mentally?

Food for Thought

Grocery shopping has never seemed as important as when you're carrying a person inside you. Every bite you choose becomes a building block in the life of your child. It's enough to cause a gal to think twice before binging on a bag of Oreos. Finally, the words we've been taught take on a new meaning: "We are what we eat, and so are our babies."

While you grow a baby, every bite transmits through your body to your growing infant. The chain goes a step further than farm to table or fork to mouth; now a mom adds "to baby." Mothers-to-be who never managed to keep up a vitamin regimen find themselves faithful in their daily pre-natal and pregnancy supplements.

Girlfriends who never checked ingredient labels start reviewing additives with the same care they give to making a baby registry. Choices made with fingers crossed often produce heartburn, extra gas, and bloating that make an expectant mom sorry she took a risk. Words like "folic acid" start popping up over dinner conversations with daddy-to-be, and caffeinated drinks get frowned on like a can of paint. No one wants to shape a new life with bad ingredients.

While nursing a baby, new moms learn quickly what foods produce negative results. There's no arguing that a mom's nutrition goes directly to a new babe when parents have an infant's tummy upset, gas drops, and toxic bowel movements to contend with. As if nine months of a total body makeover didn't make the point, a nursing baby screams loud and clear that her comfort and growth reflect the choices of her parents.

God planned for us to enjoy a feast of good foods. He invited us to set healthy habits, saying, "Behold, I have given you every plant yielding seed that is on the face of all the earth, and every tree with seed in its fruit. You shall have them for food," (Genesis 1:29). He invites us to fill the family table with all our bodies need to thrive.

While you're training a baby, a new mom may be lulled into imagining her nutrition has become her own business again. Ever watchful, a small child's world revolves around his parents, with mom in the center. The dietary example a mother models paves the way for a child to learn habits of healthy eating. If a mom turns up her nose at veggies, her child will most likely grow to join her in the snub. If a mother guzzles soda as her beverage of choice, her child will be likely to cry for carbonation.

A wise mom recognizes when her child fails to thrive physically and otherwise. If the scale shows a lack of weight gain, she seeks out help to find the cause and chooses a plan to meet the need. When nutrition is weak, a new course may need to be served, or a supplement may be added.

Children watch what their mommy feeds her body and her spirit. As he develops, the watchful child notices if mom chooses to partake of clean sources of entertainment, to consume a balanced diet of media, to digest a daily dose of truth, and to hydrate herself with the Living Water. As a child watches her mother model healthy nutrition in every way, she learns to choose from the same plate full of good choices.

A mother's nutrition becomes the menu from which her child chooses. We really are what we eat, in every way, and so are our children.

Words to grow your heart

"Every moving thing that lives shall be food for you. And as I gave you the green plants, I give you everything." (Genesis 9:3)

"Jesus said to them, 'I am the bread of life; whoever comes to me shall not hunger, and whoever believes in me shall never thirst.'" (John 6:35)

Thoughts to treasure in your heart or share with a friend

- ∞ What nutritional guidelines are you following while you are pregnant? Are there changes that are hard for you?
- ∞ What would you like your child's nutrition habits to be like? Have you talked about this with your spouse?
- ∞ What are you doing to feed yourself spiritually as a mother?

Moments of Doubt

Why do moms in catalogues and on websites look like mommy-hood is such a piece of cake? It only takes one morning in a power struggle with a toddler to leave us feeling like we don't have what it takes to be called "Mommy." Even the most maternal among us may not feel up to the task after repeated nights of on-demand feeding every two hours. After all, no one goes through an interview, takes a test, or earns a degree to become a parent. Every mother has moments of wondering if she was really meant to be a mother.

Some become moms through non-traditional means, requiring classes, a home study, and an application to foster or adopt. Tantrums and attitudes encountered by these moms may look the same as those conjured up by biological children for their moms, but non-traditional moms may also question their fitness for their new role, even after all the official requirements and preparation.

Whether she receives children through the birth canal or by another means, every mother has moments of doubt. "Can I do this? Did God make a mistake? Will I ever get this right?" Since motherhood stretches us in every way, like a belly full of quadruplets, a woman encounters her own weakness on the battleground of raising children.

How do we respond to our doubts and replace them with confidence?

Be truthful with yourself, "and you will know the truth, and the truth will set you free," (John 8:32).

∞ You feel overwhelmed by your role, because it is overwhelming.
∞ You feel weak and imperfect, because you are.
∞ You feel the need for help, because you should have help.

Tell yourself the truth. Tell your spouse the truth. Don't even be afraid to tell your little one the truth. Acknowledging the truth gives us freedom from striving for something we are not meant to achieve. Real mothering happens out of the uncertainties and hardships of days and nights of caring for someone who needs you, doesn't know what he wants, and resists being trained. It isn't always picture perfect, but you can do it.

The answer to being overwhelmed, weak, and in need of help is the strength of our perfect Parent, our Father. The Heavenly Father understands what it is to care for someone who needs Him, doesn't know what she wants, and resists being trained. He doesn't expect mothers to be perfect and doesn't cast aside those who are flawed or failing. Instead, He strengthens and helps them, gives them wisdom and refreshes them. Like a mother reaching out to an over-tired child needing to be put to bed, our Heavenly Father opens His arms to us with His promise of comfort.

∞ If we're really tired, we need to go to Him to find real rest.
∞ If we don't know what to do, we need to ask Him and get wisdom.
∞ If we feel inadequate, we need to concentrate on His sufficiency.

If you sometimes feel doubtful that you should have been entrusted with the life of a little one, be comforted to know we all feel that way sometimes. After all, being a mom is a big job. Without the help of a tender and strong Heavenly Father who always understands our needs and knows what to do, the mommy-job would be too big for us. But be confident that if He has given you a child to nurture, He can give you the energy and wisdom and desire to raise that child well.

You *can* do all things through Christ who strengthens you, and that includes being a great mom.

Words to grow your heart

"Come to me, all you who labor and are heavy laden,
and I will give you rest." (Matthew 11:28)

**Thoughts to treasure in your heart or share with a
friend**

- ∞ Is there a specific area that makes you worry you
  will not be adequate as a mom?
- ∞ When you're tired, it's easy to leave God out.
  What's one way you can spend time with Him?
- ∞ When are you most vulnerable to mommy-doubt?
  Ask God to be especially strong for you in those
  moments.

Strengthening Your Heart

Expecting Stretch Marks

During the forty weeks of pregnancy, a woman's body
goes through changes she never imagined it could.
It begs for us to use the word *miracle* to describe the
whole, amazing process. When our skin stretches more
than it's happy to, reddish or purplish marks develop
that remind me of childhood poison ivy moments,
minus the scratching. Primarily due to heredity, stretch

marks may appear on your stomach, chest, or behind, anywhere the body is doing the miraculous work of growing to accommodate carrying and bearing new life. They appear gradually, so you may not even notice them at first or even until after delivery.

Eventually, discolorations usually fade to more gray, whitish, or skin-colored tones, but a well-trained mommy eye usually knows where her marks are. Lotions and oils and creams relieve some of the pregnancy itchiness expectant moms encounter, but they really are no match for the need our skin has to stretch to do great things. Becoming a mom requires that we expand in every way.

For the first season of our lives, we mainly think about ourselves. Marriage stretches us to let go of our own desires and blend with another person, but bearing a child takes it to a whole new level. We yield our schedules, our pleasures, and our expectations to the needs of another—we let go of a lot. Not as obvious as changes on thighs or abs, the greatest changes take place in the heart and mind of a woman.

Emotionally, mentally, and physically, our lives bear the *stretch marks* of being miraculously changed as a woman, to become the mother God calls us to be. It's a gradual process of expanding our hearts to put someone else first, to add the needs of our child before our own, and to bear the weight of their life over ours. Such love stretches a marriage. Such love stretches a mother. In the moments when we feel like we cannot stretch any more without popping emotionally, mentally, or physically,

God reminds us, "My grace is sufficient for you. For power is perfected in weakness," (2 Corinthians 12:9).

Expect *stretch marks* in the process of becoming a mother, before and after delivery, but not all stretch marks are hereditary. The stretching of our lives is unique to each mother, and God invites us to generously massage the salve of His healing balm of grace and encouragement into the moments when we strain. The stretching will leave marks, but they will be beautiful evidence of God's work in the life of someone He calls to become a mommy.

Words to grow your heart

"My grace is sufficient for you. For power is perfected in weakness." (2 Corinthians 12:9)

Thoughts to treasure in your heart or share with a friend

- ∞ How is God stretching you or how has He stretched you to grow into a mom?
- ∞ What change has left a *stretch mark* in your life?

Mommy Makeover

Have you started taking pictures to chronicle the changes you're going through? Maybe you hold up a sign saying

"3 months" in front of your tiny baby bump, knowing the sign will one day be dwarfed by your magnificent belly. A mother's body experiences astounding changes as she becomes the safe place for her baby to grow and develop, an incubator perfectly formed to provide everything needed for new life to take shape.

Before the test even confirms her hopes or suspicions, a woman's body may start to feel sensations or pulsing in each area working to create and feed life. For women who never had to worry about a support bra, they may feel their breasts begin to grow right away. Hipless gals may watch as they add some extra padding and grow slightly wider to bear a baby's weight and get ready for delivery. It takes a total transformation of a woman's body to grow a baby.

It also takes a total transformation of a woman's heart to grow a mom. There is no test to see if we are ready to give up sleep, carry someone else's things, sacrifice our signature fragrance, or deal gracefully with interruptions. During the months of carrying a baby inside, we begin the change of heart and mind it takes to become a mother. Every day after the baby's arrival we gain strength in mommy boot camp, learning what to hang on to and what to push aside in order to be the kind of parent who puts her child's needs above her own. We need the divinely given portion of wisdom God bestows on moms.

Only total physical transformation produces a baby. Only total transformation in every other way produces a good mother. Instead of feeling overwhelmed at what motherhood takes, be encouraged. God promises He is the great Transformer of our hearts and lives, since "He who began a good work in you will bring it to completion at the day of Jesus Christ," (Phil. 1:6).

Like a loving parent, He will gently nurture us and keep providing for us until we are mature and complete. He will conduct the mommy makeover growing us into the mothers we need to be. We only need to offer Him our hearts and minds and behaviors and trust Him to shape us into a beautiful mom. When we fail, and we will fail, we trust that His mercies are new every morning (Lamentations 3:22-23). When we confess our failures, He forgives and keeps doing His work of transformation in us.

I've always wanted to have a total makeover. Have you? When you found out you were going to be a mommy, it began! You're going to be beautiful.

Words to grow your heart

"And I am sure of this, that he who began a good work in you will bring it to completion at the day of Jesus Christ." (Philippians 1:6)

Thoughts to treasure in your heart or share with a friend

- ∞ What were the first physical signs of change in your body?
- ∞ Are you aware of any ways God is transforming

your personality, thoughts, or habits?

∞ God wants you to keep growing up to be a mature mom. Thank Him for His commitment to do a total makeover.

Drain the Tub

What girl doesn't love a long hot bubble bath? It's right up there with a pedicure, a latte, and reading on the beach. Read a magazine and drink a latte, while getting a pedicure at the beach, and you've hit gold! A girl has to know where to re-charge on those days when work is long and the pay doesn't come close to our value. So how will you cope when every day is long and the pay can never match your value? Every mommy has to answer that question. Should I just drain the bath tub now and kiss long baths goodbye? Yes.

And no. Even Jesus modeled a pattern of getting away to a quiet place when He had been doing the work of giving to others without a break. His getaways did not include foot care, coffee, bubbles, magazines, or chocolate, but He went away to be refreshed. A worn out mommy doesn't have much to give, so she has to find ways to refresh her body and her spirit. Children need to learn early Mommy needs time to rest and be with Jesus, so she can be the best mommy she can be. And that's when you drain the bath tub.

Mothering requires putting the needs of others before

your own, setting aside your own desires to meet theirs, and taking on the role of a servant. A servant chooses to care for someone else, unlike a slave who is forced. Servants offer service willingly, but that means giving up something to make the offering. Jesus modeled a pattern of serving. He "made himself nothing, taking the form of a servant . . ." (Phil 2:7). It takes humility and obedience to give your life for another. It took daily follow-through of the decision He had made. He served us so we could live.

Out of love, a mother humbles herself and chooses to serve. No longer does she insist that indulgences in her day are necessities; they are offered up in order to serve. No longer does she require that her wants have to be paid for and fulfilled; she puts her own pleasures after the pleasure of others. No longer does she do the diva dance of getting her way; she yields it to make her child's needs greater than her own. It takes humility and obedience in daily follow-through of her decision to have a child.

But don't put away your bubbles and your back scrubber just yet. Those long bubble baths may be less frequent and shorter for a while, but they still need to happen. Sometimes the most loving thing you can do for your child is allow yourself to rest.

Remember that the greatest Servant went away to rest. His people waited, and your little one can too. Share your need with your husband, get a babysitter, find a mother's helper, ask a mentor, swap with a friend—make time for peace a priority. A peaceful mother is a better mother.

And when you steal away into the tub, take a latte

and a magazine and some chocolate for while you're soaking. A mom has to make the most of her opportunities, and you're going to be awesome at it!

Words to grow your heart

"Whoever brings blessing will be enriched, and one who waters will himself be watered." (Proverbs 11:25)

Thoughts to treasure in your heart or share with a friend

- ∞ What were your favorite ways of refreshing yourself in the pre-baby season of life?
- ∞ Have you shared your R&R loves with your mate? Does he know what you need?
- ∞ How can you plan ahead now to make occasional *Mommy R&R* part of your life?

Test Results and Testing

She handed them several brochures in muted colors, as if the contents wouldn't tear at their hearts and attention. Without looking up, the nurse listed tests the doctor had already ordered, made notes on her chart, said she would call in a week with results, and smiled momentarily, like a period on a sentence. She opened the door and walked out; the parents to be suddenly felt unsure about where the hallway would take them. The outcome of the tests could change everything.

Man's medical knowledge exceeds our wisdom to use the available insight. Sometimes limited and potentially flawed information robs a mother of her joy and expectation as she awaits her newborn's arrival. Healthcare providers may order tests as routine procedure, without a patient's consent, but parents carry the weight of the results. Most tests require time to report conclusions, making the already difficult wait of pregnancy more difficult.

Choosing what tests are ordered may be partly within a mom's control, but choosing the outcome is out of her hands. Sometimes test results have the power to produce emotional testing. When medical personnel look to parents for decisions, expectant moms and dads find their hearts overwhelmed. Questions plague new parents: *Will our child be healthy? Will our child live? Will our child be all we've dreamed of? What should we do? What does this mean? Are the tests right?* There is a place to turn when our hearts face anxiety born from the medical tests of pregnancy.

"Hear my cry, O God, listen to my prayer; from the end of the earth I call to you when my heart is faint. Lead me to the rock that is higher than I." (Psalm 61:1-2)

Only God loves your baby more than you do. While the wisdom of man offers tests and evaluations to take back control of the unpredictable nature of birthing a baby, only God knows and controls new life. Let the sovereign compassion of your Heavenly Father answer any anxiety about your own precious child.

Already, you're falling in love with your little one. Brochures and test results and information won't change that. Your heart has been captured, and captured hearts sometimes grow faint and overwhelmed.

As a little child hides her face into the comforting side of a trusted parent, so run to the Father-rock who is your refuge. He will give you wisdom to make decisions, peace about the future, and strength in the waiting. He will see you through the testing of your pregnancy.

Words to grow your heart

"Even though I walk through the valley of the shadow of death, I will fear no evil, for you are with me; your rod and your staff, they comfort me." (Psalm 23:4)

Thoughts to treasure in your heart or share with a friend

- ∞ Have you informed yourself about the regular tests of pregnancy? Don't be taken by surprise.
- ∞ What does your doctor believe about the sanctity of life? Pray for your doctor to have wisdom.
- ∞ Who will you talk to if you need to make decisions during your pregnancy? Ask God to show you who has godly insight.
- ∞ Tell the Lord your fears and pray Psalm 23:4 out loud to Him.

Getting on a Schedule

How do you feel about a schedule for your baby? Do you think you'll be the kind of mama to feed your baby like clockwork, knowing just when to wake her up and when to lay her down? Or do you think you'll feed on demand and sleep when you can? Or have you accepted that your best intentions and plans may be completely hijacked by a tiny cooing person covered in peach fuzz?

Basic needs must be met for sleeping, feeding, and learning about the world so you lay a firm foundation for your child's lifetime of good health. Most parents start out with a game plan and then modify it to fit what they learn about their baby and about themselves as they get to know each other.

How do you feel about a schedule for yourself? A mother has basic needs of her own that must be met in order to grow into mommy-hood and lay a firm foundation for a lifetime of good parenting. She needs filling of her spirit, feeding of her heart, and finding of wisdom for her new world experiencing so much change. During the months of growing a baby and then adjusting to baby's life outside the womb, a mother cannot leave out God's Word, any more than a baby could leave out human touch and milk.

More than ever before, you need an intimate relationship with your wise and loving Abba, Father. The enemy would love an opportunity to discourage, depress, and disable you in your new role as a parent. A mother starved of bonding with God and His truth will quickly show signs of mommy malnutrition and will stop thriving.

Whether you set a rigid schedule and meet with the Lord like clockwork, or *feed on demand* in whatever moments you can steal away, it's critical for a mother to plan for how she will begin or sustain patterns of worship and prayer to nurture lifetime habits of intimacy with God. Once you develop a plan, be prepared to adjust your plans when the cooing, peach fuzz covered person hijacks your quiet time too! Like so much of life in this season, your devotional time with the Lord can take on a whole new look:

∞ Listen to an audio Bible or praise music while you walk, rock the baby, or work.
∞ Memorize passages by hanging them on cabinets or over a changing table; speak them out loud. Your baby will love it. You'll lay the groundwork for hiding God's Word in his heart.
∞ Talk your devotions out loud to your baby. She will love the sound of your voice, and teaching it to someone else makes it more alive in your own heart and mind.
∞ Pray out loud with your baby. Let him hear you call out to God from his earliest days.
∞ Faithfully attend church. You need to worship with others, and your baby will be healthier if you are committed to fellowship.
∞ Keep a Bible in handy places like a diaper bag,

nightstand, bathroom, or car for unplanned quiet moments.

∞ Start a journal of thanksgiving to be a record of God's work in your life as a mother. Pray with gratitude.

∞ Let friends and others help provide a little mommy time for you, so you can refill your soul and come back ready to be a great mama.

Whether you feed on demand or schedule feedings, you would not even entertain the thought of depriving your baby of food to grow on. Don't entertain the thought of not feeding yourself as a mother. Feed regularly, feed often, and feed good quality time with God. Especially now, set healthy lifetime habits of intimacy with your Heavenly Father, letting Him nurture and strengthen you to be the best mother you can be.

Words to grow your heart

"And let us consider how to stir up one another to love and good works, not neglecting to meet together, as is the habit of some, but encouraging one another, and all the more as you see the Day drawing near."
(Hebrews 10:24-25)

Thoughts to treasure in your heart or share with a friend

∞ What have your devotional habits been like before having a baby?

∞ What strategies do you think might be best for you to feed on God's Word and have time with Him once your baby arrives?

OTHER GROWN UPS

Staying in Love

Baby Takes Two

As a baby takes up more womb space, a mom-to-be takes up more bed space. She also takes up more focus of conversation, more time at doctor's appointments, and more cash in the budget. Another person has taken over her body for nine months, so doesn't it make sense she should take center stage? If she isn't careful, she'll turn into a diva with a diaper bag. Since it took two to make a baby, no expectant mom should forget there's a daddy involved.

Because he isn't popping pre-natal vitamins, having late night cravings, running to the bathroom, or wearing a new genre of fashion, it can be easy to forget daddy's life is changing, too. His body isn't undergoing a transformation, yet a first time father experiences unseen dramatic changes. While a mother feels the weight of a growing baby inside, a father feels the weight of growing responsibility. Beyond finances, a father wonders if he can meet his wife's emotional needs, be a good father, and pay for college. You might not see his *stretch marks*, but a father stretches too. It takes two to make a baby.

A baby is a blessing for a man and wife who are one. "Like arrows in the hand of a warrior are the children of one's youth," (Psalm 127:4). One way God blesses marriage is with children. A dad feels a sense of pride in his wife's conception; her growing belly is evidence of their fruitfulness as a couple. Watch a man's chest stick out as his wife's belly sticks out. He rejoices to know his family is blessed.

Along with joy, he also feels uncertainty. (Sounds a lot like the mom-to-be.) Though most men are wired to fix problems, they realize they won't be able to fix coming issues like labor pains and crying babies. He is entering new territory, and he knows it. Unfortunately, he may not feel the same freedom to read up on baby care, ask questions to experienced dads at the office, or join online forums. Though they may want to prepare, without the benefit of a growing belly to prove they are in imminent need of answers, dads often get left out.

Dads feel blessed, and dads want to prepare, but when it comes to prepping a nursery and having a shower, dads get left out in the waiting room. This is not to say dads need to learn to love tiny pink and blue cupcakes and make diaper cakes. A wise expectant mom encourages her expectant daddy to share his thoughts and prepare in his own way, in his daddy way. Can he build something for baby's room? Would he like to buy baby's first sports jersey? Does he want to be the official belly photographer? Welcome his participation in his daddy ways.

How has God designed your expectant husband to anticipate and prepare for your coming baby? Your child is a gift from God, a blessing on your marriage, and an arrow in the hand of your warrior. You're not so big that you need to take up the whole center of the stage yourself. After all, it took two to make your baby, so you should share the spotlight.

Words to grow your heart

> "The father of the righteous will greatly rejoice;
> he who fathers a wise son will be glad in him."
> (Proverbs 23:24)

Thoughts to treasure in your heart or share with a friend

- ∞ Other than conception, how has your husband been involved in your pregnancy so far?
- ∞ How can you invite and encourage your husband to use his particular personality, interests, and skills to prepare for baby coming?

A Bigger Flying Carpet

While riding on a flying carpet for two, Aladdin sang to his beloved Jasmine, "I can show you the world . . ." When the harmony reaches its peak and the two lock eyes, it's one of those priceless moments we all hope for. We're realistic about the flying carpet, but we want to know the thrill of our Prince Charming sweeping us away to show us the world. It sets us both up for disappointment and confusion when we find ourselves too pregnant to fit on a flying carpet and too tired to care about seeing the world. When a baby comes into your fairy tale, the relationship with your prince changes. Why didn't they show us that part in the movie?

Knowing there is as baby inside you, made by the two of you, is exhilarating. There's something intimate and sacred about carrying the child of your lover, and your husband feels the same, knowing his child is inside of you. While the miracle draws you closer in some ways, it may also push you apart if you are not aware of the changes in your relationship.

With so much changing about your body, expectant moms and dads may be nervous or uncomfortable about how to be physically close under the new circumstances. You begin to see yourselves as a mommy and a daddy instead of just two lovers. Passion moves to a new place as you learn how to express your love for each other in different ways from those that came so naturally when you fit on a flying carpet for two. Touching and experiencing your growing belly with a baby's movement inside may replace the first touching you enjoyed in your unseasoned love. A man must live with his wife "in an understanding way," (1 Peter 3:7), and a wife must "see that she respect her husband," (Ephesians 5:33). This is a time to work at understanding and respecting each other, taking on a whole new world of greater understanding, communication, and unselfishness.

By sharing your feelings honestly and inviting your mate to share openly about his feelings, you move through the parenting transformation together. Instead of letting the one flesh relationship that made your baby become consumed by the pregnancy, keep your conversation and care for each other varied. Talk and think about more than just the baby. As you do, you prepare fertile ground for your baby to be born into a healthy family, led by parents who grow together in each season of married life.

Parenthood changes the relationship with your prince, but the changes can make the ride together even sweeter as you experience life together. Don't give in to the temptation to stay on the ground, insist you don't want to see the world, and claim it's not good for the baby. That kind of an attitude makes an expectant father feel like he's gaining a baby, but losing his lover.

A mother who nurtures a growing, changing relationship with her husband is good for a baby. Like your first season of love, parenting has a harmony all its own. You don't need to get rid of that flying carpet, just get one that's family size. Children change life for lovers, but they don't need to crush it.

Words to grow your heart

"In the same way husbands should love their wives as their own bodies. He who loves his wife loves himself . . . However, let each one of you love his wife as himself, and let the wife see that she respects her husband." (Ephesians 5:28, 33)

Thoughts to treasure in your heart or share with a friend

- ∞ Be honest. On a scale of one to ten, how much of your relationship with your husband revolves around your coming baby?
- ∞ What's a way you and your man spend time enjoying life together?
- ∞ How can you plan for some me-and-my-man time to nurture your relationship?

A Not-so-hostile Takeover

Tiny and helpless. Unable to feed themselves or lift their heads. How can someone so small be so powerful? They capture our hearts, dominate our energy, control our time, and steal our love, yet they look so innocent. We gladly give it all to them in the amazing wonder of becoming a parent.

Families begin with vows to love, honor, and cherish; two are declared to be one flesh, pronouncing that no one should separate them. Who would anticipate that an infant could be a wedge between a husband and wife? Sometimes they are. In a couple's efforts to devote themselves to the care and nurture of the child they share, parents may sabotage the very foundation they built. If a child is to have a healthy understanding of loving and being loved, he can't be number one in his home.

A mother may find herself with mixed emotions here, because her baby lives and grows inside her own body for nine months. She may feel like she and her child are united. While God prepares her to carry the baby, He doesn't prepare her to become one with her child. From cutting the cord to delivering the amniotic sac to weaning from breast milk, the physical process of birth reminds a mother she carries and delivers her child so they can live on their own.

A mother is one with her husband. Together, they raise their child to independence. Since a baby brings the need for constant care, a lot of equipment, and a claim on his mother's body, parents have to be intentional about not letting a child become the king or queen of their castle. Differences in opinion about child rearing and about the changes in their lives may threaten to divide a couple who is not watching for divisions threatening to separate them. Without keeping the marriage relationship as the center of their home, a baby will gladly take over and enjoy being number one.

Since they have such power to melt our hearts with a single coo and control us with a brief yawn, how do we guard against a babe's not-so-hostile takeover? Daily decisions force a mother to choose who is number one, her child or her husband.

When it is not a question of necessity, choose your husband first. As he feels secure in your love and honor, he will join you in meeting the baby's needs. A child who learns to wait grows to be unselfish and grateful. A child who knows her parents will not be separated grows secure and confident. A child who watches her parents honor each other grows up seeking respectful, loving relationships. Putting your marriage relationship first grows a happy baby.

One day your helpless babe, looking a lot like one of you, will step out as an adult to make his way in the world. You'll still wonder if he can feed himself, and you'll still melt at the sight of his smile. He'll look back on times he tried to come between you, play one against the other, or rule the household. He will be blessed to know you were inseparable and had first place in each other's hearts. You'll enjoy knowing the child God gave to your marriage made your union sweeter. Before your little royal arrives, determine to give him the place in your hearts and lives that's best for all of you: second place.

Words to grow your heart

"Therefore a man shall leave his father and mother
and hold fast to his wife, and the two shall become
one flesh. So they are no longer two but one flesh.
What therefore God has joined together, let no man
separate." (Mark 10:7-9)

Thoughts to treasure in your heart or share with a friend

∞ What did you vow to your husband when the two of you became a family?
∞ Do you have dreams for what your life will be like

together when your children are grown?

∞ What kind of marriage do you want your children to see modeled for them?

Let's Get Physical . . . Again

Do you know what moment you conceived your baby? If it was natural, you might have a romantic evening, a vacation setting, a quiet night, or a sleepy Saturday morning to remember. Others might think back to a doctor's office and a procedure surrounded by hope, after many times of trying and praying for sweet intimacy to result in a sweet baby.

Think back even further to when your sexual oneness was new and unfamiliar, exciting and unreserved. Does it seem like a long time ago? You're not alone if stretch marks, indigestion, weight gain, ultrasounds, prenatal visits, and hormones have pushed memories of love making into the fog of your memory. Expectant women may experience lustful urges in their pregnant state, or they might find themselves doing battle with fears about hurting their unborn children.

Whatever the size of the babe within, knowing there is a child inside you and between you will change your physical intimacy. Once a baby emerges, knowing there is a child in the next room will change your physical intimacy. Is it really that important or even possible to get physical again?

Experiencing the birth of your child together brings a couple closer than ever before. The nine months of gestation provide a sweet season for a husband and wife to prepare for their new roles together as mom and dad. It's not a time to retreat to their own corners in isolation, though hormones may whisper that suggestion to an expectant mom. Just as a decision was made to share life together and to become parents, so a decision must be made to be close, physically and emotionally.

A husband is so much more to a wife than a means of being impregnated, yet some waiting mothers may leave waiting fathers feeling like they are of no use. Even in pregnancy, a man and wife are still, first of all, man and wife. They are both called to look out for the needs of the other, to care for each other, to know and be known, and to love each other. While their arsenal of affection may change, the need to meet each other's needs does not. Especially during a season of change and newness, a husband also needs to feel loved, secure, appreciated, and desired for more than his help in bearing the babe, making late night restaurant runs, or carrying shower gifts.

As an expectant woman's body grows, she may find new ways to show her husband her love for him, to express her desire to be close to him, and to allow him to enjoy her pregnant beauty. Bearing a child does not take a woman away from her man and give her to a child; bearing a child takes a woman and bonds her to her man in a new way.

Depending on the delivery process, getting physical again may take time, patience, and open communication. Physical healing might make the reconnection awkward or uncomfortable. Help each other understand your needs. Do not let the wonder of parenthood keep you from enjoying the spouse whose love produced your child.

Find comfort and pleasure and love in the arms of the father of your child. After all, first he is your husband.

Words to grow your heart

"Many waters cannot quench love, neither can floods drown it." (Song of Solomon 8:7a)

Thoughts to treasure in your heart or share with a friend

- ∞ What inhibitions or concerns do you have about intimacy while pregnant?
- ∞ Describe what speaks love to your husband and makes him feel appreciated.
- ∞ How can you plan to spend time together just enjoying and focusing on each other?

Baby Talk about Daddy

It will begin as coos and morph slowly into single syllables before it begins to be connected into words able to melt your heart. Baby talk. The language development of your small one will fascinate and delight you as you hear the unique sound of her voice and imprint it on your heart and mind. While you are absorbing the precious first words, she will be absorbing all of yours.

The tiny, fuzz outlined ears will bounce each sound wave into your child's memory and understanding, and she will learn. From your accent and your tone and your inflection, she will learn how language sounds. And from your content, she will make sense of her world and her relationships. What will you say about daddy?

Mommies market daddies. In other words, moms speak an image of daddy to their listening and learning children. We cannot help but deliver our first words spoken to baby's ears in our most gentle, love soaked words, but as the first days grow into weeks and months and years, regular life settles in and takes over our tongues. Early on, it's easy to tenderly beg, "Show Daddy your best smile. Daddy loves you and wants to see your happy face. Show Daddy how much you love him."

But as maternity leave turns into over-full days and hospital stays turn into insurance bills, miraculous days may be taken over by routine. "Oh look at this! Doesn't Daddy remember how to put on a diaper? It looks like Daddy just dumped your dinner right in your lap!"

Delight crumbles into moments of irritation, and gratitude collapses into words of criticism. As you leave rattles and onesies behind to embrace book bags and sports jerseys, the language of sarcasm and belittling may try to work its way into your conversation like a child trying to find an opening in her mama's shirt to nurse.

If we aren't careful, the language lessons we continue to teach may include disrespect toward the very daddy who grew teary eyed at the first coos and calls of your once tiny child. How will you talk to baby about daddy? Ephesians 5:33 gives us the bottom line, spelling out a gentle command for our good, like we will spell out gentle commands for the welfare of our babes; ". . . let the wife see that she respects her husband." Whether the diaper is like we want it, the food is where we direct it, or the football game is the priority we hope for, we are called to respect the men who are our husbands and the fathers of our children. Little fuzzy ears will be listening to our every word, our every tone, our every intonation. They'll know the message of our hearts, and they will take it into theirs as their baby talk grows up.

Sometimes the mouth that smiles with overflowing love and speaks the first words of amazement is the same mouth that spews anger and complaining and sarcasm. "From the same mouth come blessing and cursing. My brothers, these things ought not to be so," (James 3:10).

Prepare your heart for the angelic sounds of baby talk, and prepare the heart of your child to respect and admire the father who gave her life. Teach with love from your own mouth, and be blessed by the words of respect you and your husband will hear as your baby's talk grows up.

Words to grow your heart

"The words of a man's mouth are deep waters; the fountain of wisdom is a bubbling brook."
(Proverbs 18:4)

"The words of a wise man's mouth win him favor, but the lips of a fool consume him." (Ecclesiastes 10:12)

Thoughts to treasure in your heart or share with a friend

- ∞ Describe how you would want your child to finish this sentence: "When my mom talks, it's like she . . ."
- ∞ What kind of respectful words will you use to talk about your husband to your child?
- ∞ When you have moments of frustration, what would be other ways to address the issues, besides blurting out negativity and disrespect in front of or to your child?

Nurturing Your Relationships

Your Family in Your Family

I carefully wrapped the milky-white soap in a paper towel, breathing in its fragrance of spring flowers and smiling at the thought of presenting the gift to my loved one. To be sure it was secure, I lodged it between other little gifts to be delivered and snacks to be consumed, arranging it with bars of granola, blocks of chocolate, packs of gum, and cracker packs. Before I closed the suitcase for the flight, I closed the plastic bag of goodies, sealing it tightly with the luxurious soap deep inside.

When we finally landed in a foreign destination, loved ones greeted us. Excited to share our gifts with them, we uncovered our bundle. To our surprise, everything sealed with the fragrant gift was infused with its aroma; nothing escaped the smell. The soapy fragrance even saturated once-delicious foods. The addition of one small item, though beautiful on its own, changed everything around it.

A baby changes the dynamic of the whole family into which she is born. Relationships, once as comfortable as worn slippers, may become awkward and troublesome, while others may feel like leather shoes finally softened and stretched to suit the foot. The mom-to-be might be the one to show off the changes, but all of the family feels the arrival of the newcomer.

A baby infuses all of family life.

Married relationships change. Before your child was born, your family was born. A one-flesh couple is a family all on their own. Family relationships closest to the brand new babe absorb the fragrance the most. Husbands and wives enter a season of change, forced to adjust their communication, their intimacy, their time together, their priorities, and their household.

Relative relationships change. A little further out from mom and dad, relationships feel the power of the small gift wrapped in a soft blanket with satin edging. Parents-in-law navigate new territory of their own, eager to be accepted and significant, excited to share their experience and wisdom, hopeful to be embraced by the grandchild they have dreamed of. Welcome their contribution and bonding with your child. Each extended family member explores their new role related to your little one and to you as a new mother; they've never known you in motherhood before. Being a family within a family takes grace and patience as everyone adjusts.

A child thrives best in a strong family within a family.

Change requires balance. With all of the adjustments, determine to be balanced in your family unit. When a mom-to-be and dad-to-be welcome a little one, their child brings greater fullness to their union. New parents are wise to recognize themselves as a family unit and to commit to standing together in parenting. As decisions start to erupt like spit-up after a feeding, new moms and dads need to strive for unity, not letting anything drive a wedge between them, even well-meaning relatives.

Balance requires boundaries. Loved ones who have longed for the arrival of your little one need grace and clarity. Instead of leaving family members wondering, talk openly about your needs. Clear boundaries provide freedom for new parents to grow into parents and for grandparents to grow into grandparents. Boundaries also provide security for your child who will need to understand each of the roles you play in his life.

Nothing stirs up the enthusiastic love of extended family members more than the arrival of a child. Mature parenting displays balance by inviting relatives to be part of a child's life, while keeping healthy boundaries for their family within the family. To allow for new families to enjoy the valuable role relatives play, while keeping each family unit sacred, God gives parents simple instructions. "Therefore a man shall leave his father and his mother and hold fast to his wife, and they shall become one flesh," (Genesis 2:24). The child they once swaddled or considered a playmate has become a mother or a father, and there's a newly born person to bond with and love. New parents grow the best families when they both believe they are a complete family unit.

Moms- and dads-to-be can welcome extended loved ones into the life of their child without letting go of their union as parents.

Words to grow your heart

"Gray hair is a crown of glory; it is gained in a righteous life." (Proverbs 16:31)

"Honor your father and your mother, that your days may be long in the land that the Lord your God is giving you." (Exodus 20:12)

Thoughts to treasure in your heart or share with a friend

∞ No extended family is perfect; what positive contributions did your family of origin make in your life?

∞ What good things may your joint extended families provide for your child?

∞ Do you anticipate any challenges as you all come together to love your child?

∞ How can you show your husband you are on the same team as a family?

Belly Bands and Bonding

When about thirty weeks have passed and wardrobe options are limited to empire waist dresses and pants with navy-blue stretchy panels, expectant moms may consider wearing a belly band for support. Wrapped around her belly full of baby, the band helps hold up the extra load in the final trimester.

Becoming a mother is a load unlike any most women have experienced. Even the most independent gals may find having a baby brings out her need to have people she loves and trusts provide support. As a mom-to-be invites the strength of others around her, they help her bear the added weight of carrying and caring for a child. Their involvement also has the potential to help lift up a child's life.

With her world changing physically, emotionally, professionally, and relationally, a first time mom may find herself overwhelmed with the new load she carries. After delivering her infant, a whole new set of needs and responsibilities add their weight to a woman's heart, mind, and time. The heaviness of the final-trimester tummy is forgotten as she adjusts to the size of the job of raising a child. Is there a belly band for a mom's heart?

No matter how much of a super-mommy a gal is, no one woman can be everything her child needs. But you don't have to be. Other people add their experiences, interests, abilities, wisdom, and love when they wrap around a child in a supportive relationship. "Again, if two lie together, they keep warm, but how can one keep warm alone?" (Ecclesiastes 4:11). A mom's life is sweeter and a child's future brighter when other people are invited in.

Mothers gain freedom and strength by welcoming the involvement of other loving adults into their children's lives. Instead of feeling like every need falls on her shoulders, she enjoys the health and balance that comes from sharing her load. Having a friend or family member support her through childcare, providing a meal, or offering companionship can make the difference between managing her new world or feeling oppressed by it. Children gain confidence and strength when they learn about other ways of doing things, know they have multiple people to count on, and feel encouraged to bond with others. In considering what is best for a little one, a wise mother gets a better return for her labor by inviting others to bond and build into the life of her child.

There will come a time when you no longer need a belly band and can see your feet without leaning over. There will never come a time when your life and that of your child's won't benefit from supportive bonds with loved ones. Invite them to wrap around your family as it grows, uphold you in the midst of the changes, and lift you up to become the mother and child God dreams for you to be.

Words to grow your heart

> "Two are better than one, because they have a good reward for their toil." (Ecclesiastes 4:9)

Thoughts to treasure in your heart or share with a friend

∞ Who are the people in your life who provide a belly band of support for you?
∞ What will the people in your life add to your child's life as she learns and grows?

Friendship

Cheerios littered the floor under the café table, and her bagel had long grown cold. Only small pieces had been torn out of the dough in my girlfriend's attempts to feed her busy babe who sat in the highchair like a throne. He would suck on the pieces until they resembled Play-Doh, then stick them randomly on his mommy's purse, shoulder, or cheek. We finally surrendered, gathered the gear, and stepped through cereal crumbs to escape the bakery. Behind us sat quiet adults drinking their coffee and frowning at the evidence we left behind.

Reaching her car, we spied her stroller jammed between a box of diapers and the door of the mini-van. Thinking it might be the answer to mommy-time with a friend, we strapped in the Cheerios-chucking babe and started our first lap around the parking lot. It can be a lot of work to have friendships when a baby is in the picture, so is it worth it?

Even a mama needs a friend. Since one of the hazards of new-mama days may be a feeling of isolation, especially a mama needs a friend. Women go to a lot of trouble to arrange playdates for growing toddlers, and they understand their guy needs a guy's night out, but the mom journey will be a happier, healthier adventure when a mommy makes friendship a priority for herself. A husband may be a partner and a lover, and a baby may be the light of your lives together, but Mommy needs a girlfriend, too.

In the midst of all the changes in a woman's life, it's important to keep friends you have. "A friend loves at all times, and a brother is born for adversity," (Proverbs 17:17). A mom is blessed to have a friend who will love her as she changes and as her life changes and as she faces the adversity motherhood brings. Instead of letting old friends go the way of hour long soaks in the tub and sleeping late on Saturdays, keep the friendships you have cherished close to your heart. Your time together may look different, but if you need to do laps in the parking lot to spend time together, start walking! Mommy needs to keep her friends.

A friend loves at all times, even if her milk is leaking and she hasn't had a shower in three days. New moms might feel like being a friend to someone else is just more than they can manage, yet a wise woman remembers to consider those around her on her motherhood journey. Every mama reaches a time when she feels overwhelmed with all of the *new*, but mothers who do not forsake their friends and distance themselves during the hard times will be grateful for the rare quality of friendship they discover in time. "Do not forsake your friend and your father's friend, and do not go to your brother's house in the day of your calamity. Better is a neighbor who is near than a brother who is far away," (Proverbs 27:10). Mommy needs to be a good friend.

Motherhood is the door to a whole new world. In addition to a relationship with the newly born member of the family, motherhood introduces a woman to other travelers on the parenting journey. Parents at playgrounds, libraries, small groups, and nurseries find each other and share their common story. Other relationships may blossom in the form of a mentor, babysitter, or teacher, where once nothing grew. The Heavenly Father still delights in showering His sweet girls with blessings during motherhood, just as a loving parent arranges a playdate with a friend who will be a joy to her little loved one. "If you then, who are evil, know how to give good gifts to your children, how much more will your Father who is in heaven give good things to those who ask him!" (Matthew 7:11). Mommy needs to receive new friends.

A mother's heart may be full with affection for her babe, but she will be a healthier, happier mama if she's a good friend who cares for her friendships and nurtures the gift of new ones. A good friend will love at all times, especially in the baby times.

Words to grow your heart

"Many a man proclaims his own steadfast love, but a faithful man who can find?" (Proverbs 20:6)

Thoughts to treasure in your heart or share with a friend

- ∞ How has welcoming a child into your life changed your friendships for the good?
- ∞ How has expecting or welcoming a child into your life challenged your friendships?
- ∞ What new ways can you spend time with your friends and keep up your connection?

Keeping a Wide-angle Lens

We all swarmed around the counter covered with food, mostly made from first time recipes in kitchens with baking sheets still clean and silver. The couples chattered about their week and migrated to the living room with their plates and cups. One pair smiled broadly with a twinkle in their eyes, suggesting they had news to tell. Before long, her eyes met his, and their hands linked together. He cleared his throat, as if stepping up on stage to make a great announcement.

Only the two of us, having once linked hands in just the same way and spoken the announcement in the same way, knew what was about to be pronounced. They were having a baby.

Cries of joy and smiles of blessing exploded in the room like the first rain drops in a spring deluge. They giggled and shared, and we all rejoiced. But it was not easy for everyone. For some in the room, they offered congratulations while the room spun and knots formed in their stomachs, as tears demanded to flow and questions begged to be answered.

One friend had privately endured a miscarriage, and she wrestled with grief too fresh to share it. Another longed to conceive a child, logging hours in medical appointments and more in prayer. The youngest looked hopefully to when she would have the joy of making a pronouncement, but her husband was holding firm to financial preparation. Amid the intentional and sincere hugs and the smiles, no one stole any of the joy of the expectant couple, but pain rippled beneath the surface for some.

The journey of mothering gives us the experience we need to comfort others.

To expect the arrival of a child is to understand what it is to have pain. Whatever the nature of her particular struggle, from complications to contractions, a woman gains awareness of how others hurt. As she takes profile pictures of her growing belly, moves to the first hospital photos, and then shares professional baby photos with friends, it is easy to fall into viewing life with a narrow lens. While longing for, carrying, bearing, and raising a child, a mother must use her new awareness to keep looking through a wide-angle lens.

With all the joy that comes with a new baby, what mom doesn't find herself captivated and consumed by the little person who demands to be the center of her world? With their smells and sounds and momentous achievements, who can blame a new mother when the eyes of her heart see only the miracle called "our child"? Yet with the discovery of her own gift, others around her may be hurting, longing, or healing, and her decision to keep her perspective wide enough to see them will bless the friends and acquaintances who give her the gift of choosing to celebrate.

Words to grow your heart

"Blessed be the God and Father of our Lord Jesus Christ, the Father of mercies and God of all comfort, who comforts us in all our affliction, so that we may be able to comfort those who are in any affliction, with the comfort with which we ourselves are comforted by God. For as we share abundantly in Christ's sufferings, so through Christ we share abundantly in comfort too." (2 Corinthians 1:3-5)

Thoughts to treasure in your heart or share with a friend

- ∞ How would you describe any hardships your mothering journey has included?
- ∞ Who do you see through your life's lens who may be in a hard place as a mom-to-be?
- ∞ Did you encounter anyone who was hurtful as you awaited a baby?
- ∞ What did people do or say that was helpful to you as you waited to have a child?

Connecting Your Wires

There are more ways to connect with other women than ever before. Social media puts you in touch with friends far and near and offers you the chance to make new connections with people who share your interests. If you find yourself entering motherhood without an older relative nearby, technology provides solutions for that too; some families even share the birthing room via Skype. Websites offer mentoring wisdom for women taking their first steps on the path of parenting. With all these wired ways to connect, moms should never feel alone. Right?

When a woman's life stretches into motherhood, there's no substitute for another real woman.

If a mom-to-be experiences symptoms of distress,

the doctor wants a hands-on, in the room, eye-to-eye checkup to know the condition of mom and baby. Information over the phone may be incomplete or misunderstood. There's no substitute for physical presence.

With all of the platforms to keep from feeling isolated, the temptation may be to post a message to the world that makes it sounds like you are a rock star in transitioning to motherhood. Relatives and friends may see pictures of your cherub and read professions of your adoration and leave feeling glad you've got this mommy thing down without any trouble.

Meanwhile, the reality may be that you were up half the night, have not had a shower, are not sure what position the baby should sleep in, and your husband feels left out. Reaching out to the wired world might keep you at a safe distance from too much exposure or input, but it may also rob you of one of God's greatest gifts in motherhood: sisterhood.

Sisterhood happens with women older, in the same stage of life, and even younger than you are. It happens when the things of life expose a woman's weakness, leaving her open and eager for another woman's friendship. As we share the burden of bearing children into life and raising them up, women share wisdom and advice, prayer and encouragement, empathy and companionship. They also share a cup of coffee, a meal, a hug, or some energy to change one more diaper or wipe one more nose.

God has given every woman gifts to bless others; "As each has received a gift, use it to serve one another, as good stewards of God's varied grace," (1 Peter 4:10). The active word "serve" paints the picture of taking care of someone's needs, waiting on them domestically, and even providing food for them. This happens when we serve each other in real life. While websites may offer information, sisterhood provides a filter for real life lived by real moms with real children so women make better decisions, feel stronger, and become greater moms.

As women spend time in each other's physical presence, modeling, training, and encouraging take place. Titus 2 calls older women to be available to young women, to "teach what is good, and so train the young women . . . Show yourself in all respects to be a model of good works . . ." (Titus 2:3b-7). Hearing another woman talk to her children, watching her discipline them, and seeing how she manages her day helps a new mom know what is realistic and what works.

It may be easy and quick to hop on social media or default to call a distant relative, but God grows beauty among mothers when they seek each other out in real life. Next time you greet the morning feeling like you cannot face the day, call an older woman in your church or neighborhood and go for a walk (pushing a stroller, of course) or get a cup of coffee and tell her how you are . . . hands on, in the room, eye to eye.

When you have time on your hands and an Internet connection, resist the urge to link up every time and, instead, open your door and head out into your neighborhood. Find that other new mom who wants to connect and discover sweet sisterhood. Don't let the baby stop you; babies really are made to be mobile and relational.

You'll be a better mom if you have real relationships with real women than if you only mother in a virtual world.

Words to grow your heart

"For you were called to freedom, brothers. Only do not use your freedom as an opportunity for the flesh, but through love serve one another. For the whole law is fulfilled in one word: 'You shall love your neighbor as yourself.'" (Galatians 5:13-14)

Thoughts to treasure in your heart or share with a friend

∞ How do you communicate with your most frequent relationships with other women?

∞ Is there an older woman in your life who is able to be with you?

∞ What might be an obstacle that would make it hard to be with other women?

∞ How can you reach out to other women around you?

BABY

Designing the Nursery

The Perfect Nursery

As you choose a crib, stroller, and car seat, are you checking to see how safe they are? Are you looking for four-star items so you only get the best for your baby? New parents go to a lot of trouble to find the best equipment for their little ones. God has started their life in the perfect nursery.

The first time you hear a heartbeat, your own heart will flutter at the miracle inside you. When ultrasound pictures reveal tiny arm buds and legs or a profile taking shape, the miracle becomes more real. You'll begin to discover just how perfectly God has designed the nursery of your womb.

Psalm 139:13-16 describes a mother's womb as a secret and dark place, but a place not hidden from God's sight. Before parents-to-be ever know an infant is "being made" and "intricately woven" inside, God is on the job caring for your baby. We may think we're the first to know we're pregnant, but God has already written every one of a baby's days in His book and has already called them "wonderful." He's forming "inward parts" out of "unformed substance," knitting together your tiny loved one in a place only He can see. The Psalmist reveals how perfect and private a mother's womb is meant to be, because he wants us to know we can never be away from God's presence. He knows us and sees us whether we go to the farthest ends of the earth or to the darkest corners of the womb. A mother's body is the perfect nursery for God to form new life.

Though perfect for babies, our wombs don't house perfect people. To a new parent, studying her infant, it's easy to believe her little one was fashioned by God's hand, but the baby isn't perfect. Psalm 51:5 tells us people are "brought forth in iniquity," already imperfect in heart when we're conceived. First-time moms and dads catch glimpses of a baby's fallen nature the first time he clenches his fist in anger or spits out his peas in defiance. Even while we're in our mother's perfect nursery, God is active in our lives and working to lovingly shape us, care for us, and teach our souls to long for His touch. He places a baby in the most loving of places in the first stage of life.

Read up on the safety reports. Ask for advice from seasoned parents. Compare the facts. Choose the best equipment you can find to hold your precious bundle, but know God has already given him his start in the most perfect nursery imaginable: your womb.

Stop and praise Him for allowing you to be such a vital part of your baby's life and ask Him to guide you in carrying your baby well. And in case you're prone to forget that your very body is part of something so "fearfully and wonderfully made," go ahead and get a washable marker and draw four stars on your belly. After all, you are the very workshop where God is fashioning a new person's life!

Words to grow your heart

"For you formed my inward parts; you knitted me together in my mother's womb. I praise you, for I am fearfully and wonderfully made. Wonderful are your works; my soul knows it very well." (Psalm 139:13-14)

Thoughts to treasure in your heart or share with a friend

∞ How much do you know about what's happening inside you, biologically? Learn and be amazed!

∞ Talk with your husband or a friend about what's happening at this stage in your pregnancy. Enjoy the amazement together and give praise for the privilege of being your baby's four-star, perfect nursery!

The Heart of the Nursery

We didn't have much when we found out we were pregnant. With a husband in graduate school, our nursery needed to be the product of creativity and resourcefulness, and we needed to move it six months after our bundle arrived. It would not be the picture-perfect baby's room I had dreamed of.

Determined that our child would come to a beautiful space, I painted what I could and bought material to sew a blanket and accessories. But I'm not a seamstress. I planned to make an intricate cross-stitched wall hanging, but I'm not much of a cross-stitcher. My best attempts left the nursery looking woefully homemade and resonating with a single reminder: the beauty in our baby's world would have to come from our hearts, not our home.

Dreaming about and planning for your baby's room can be magical. In it you create a place filled with the first things of the world that you want to introduce to your babe. You carefully choose the colors and the theme and the images that will leave early imprints on your little one's mind. You nurture the beginnings of his curiosity and interests. It may also be the place you craft for spending quiet hours rocking to sleep or cranky hours pacing the floor, determined hours feeding or happy hours reading. In creating your baby's nursery, you design your child's first concept of home. What could be more important?

More than a coordinated color palette, a complete ensemble of accessories, or a cute display of a theme, your heart determines the atmosphere of your babe's home. A mom-to-be may spend time and money preparing the picture-perfect nursery, but her heart determines the tone of the room. Even a designer nursery cannot be a place of peace and beauty if the heart of the mom isn't adorned with a peaceful spirit and a lovely attitude to match.

> "The good person out of the good treasure of his heart produces good, and the evil person out of his evil treasure produces evil, for out of the abundance of the heart his mouth speaks." (Luke 6:45)

It would be so easy if new parents could just put "good heart" on their registry and expect to be handed a baby-themed gift bag with a good heart inside. Such a heart cannot be demanded or simply checked off, and it takes more time and understanding than making an intricate cross-stitched wall hanging or a lopsided quilt. But for all the effort it requires, a parent's heart filled with an abundance of good treasure is the most important piece of a baby's environment.

So if you can't register for this necessary accessory for baby's world, how do you obtain this abundance of heart?

- ∞ A good heart has been cleaned with the living water of Jesus Christ.
- ∞ A good heart puts away things that control and make us selfish.
- ∞ A good heart has God's Spirit within, bearing fruit of the Spirit.
- ∞ A good heart is careful to obey God's ways and keep His priorities.

A mother's heart cannot be silenced. Whether it's abundantly good or abundantly selfish, it will speak and be heard. Like a coat of well-coordinated paint bringing all of the details together, a mommy fills the room with words born out of her heart. More than a color scheme or stimulating visuals or a classic character or a designer ensemble, a mother's own heart is the most important part of a baby's first home.

Words to grow your heart

"I will sprinkle clean water on you, and you shall be clean from all your uncleannesses, and from all your idols I will cleanse you. And I will give you a new heart, and a new spirit I will put within you. And I will remove the heart of stone from your flesh and give you a heart of flesh. And I will put my Spirit within you, and cause you to walk in my statutes and be careful to obey my rules." (Ezekiel 36:25-27)

Thoughts to treasure in your heart or share with a friend

- ∞ What are your plans for your baby's nursery? How do you want the space to feel?
- ∞ What are your plans to prepare your heart for your baby? How do you want your baby to feel with you?
- ∞ What could you do to add abundance to your heart before your baby's arrival or as your baby grows?

Gender Reveal

Sometime in the second trimester, when your ultra-sound pictures begin to resemble Aunt Janice or Uncle Larry, you'll decide if you want to know the gender of your baby. About that time, people start making predictions based on the baby's heart rate, activity you feel, how you carry the baby, the shape of your belly, or even the cravings you experience! Some couples opt to save the gender reveal for the moment of birth, happy to have their nursery stocked with yellow and green blankets and onesies. Others want to know if their world is about to be colored pink or blue, so they can settle on a name, choose a specific nursery theme, and even do some planning for post birth plans like circumcision. Occasionally couples are split, and one may vow to keep the secret. Do you want to know long before contractions start, or do you want to savor the anticipation?

Whether it happens in a darkened ultrasound room with only two or three present or in a busy birthing room after labor, the big gender reveal is packed with excitement. The simple pronouncement of "It's a boy" or "It's a girl" is pregnant with implications for the future. Do you envision cowboy birthdays or princess parties? Will you spend hours on the bleachers of a football field or watching a dance recital? While most children choose some traditionally gender specific interests, don't be surprised if yours makes her own way on the field or blazes a trail of poetry and paintings through his school years. That's why I am blessed with a daughter who loved frogs, didn't shrink back at snakes, and could out-backpack her boyfriend. God has designed boys and girls differently, but within each gender, so much waits to be revealed.

As your little miss or mister grows up, they will need to see the fullness of God's design for a man and a woman in your example. Let them experience the amazing gender reveal throughout their lives. Man was created first and given the responsibility to work and keep the creation, but he was incomplete, (Genesis 2: 15-18). God used a rib from the first man, Adam, to shape the perfect complement to a man: a woman. She was given as a helper and partner to a man, the perfect mate. They fit together so uniquely and perfectly that their union has the ability to produce new life! A baby is born from the contribution of a man and a woman, both distinct in their parts and functions. After sin distorted the once-perfect conditions, the woman was given a name to show she is the "mother of all the living," the nurturer in a world in need of care. As we are shown in 1 Peter 3:4, God loves gentleness in a female and considers it beautiful. God plans for boys to grow into men ready to provide and protect, while He plans for girls to grow into women prepared to nurture and help. Both have great value, and a wider reading of Scripture reveals both genders are intended for strength, wisdom, boldness, and passion. Whether the world takes on a pink or a blue tone, the great gender reveal is one of understanding

God's miraculous design for a child.

You will be the first woman your child knows. Your husband will be the first man your child knows. Your life will show your child so much about your own gender and that of your spouse. Lessons from your life will imprint onto your child's heart. Are you ready for your children to have their gender and all of its beauty revealed in your footsteps? The announcement of "It's a . . ." is so exciting, but it's just the beginning of an amazing journey of discovering who they are.

Words to grow your heart

"So God created man in his own image, in the image of God he created him; male and female he created them." (Genesis 1:27)

Thoughts to treasure in your heart or share with a friend

- ∞ What new traits are you learning about yourself as a woman?
- ∞ What new qualities are you learning about your husband?
- ∞ Do you think you know what gender your child is? Have others made predictions?
- ∞ If you hear "Congratulations, it's a boy!" what will you pray for your son?
- ∞ If you hear "Congratulations, it's a girl!" what will you pray for your daughter?

Baby's Bed

Did you do your homework before you bought a crib for your little angel? No new parent would knowingly put their baby in a dangerous bed or position. We all pray and plan for perfect peace in our child's sleep world, but maybe baby's bed isn't the most important piece of the slumber puzzle.

In the first days out of the womb, most babies are champion sleepers. As they adjust to life outside their warm, wet world, they're growing at exponential rates, putting them to rest in a depth of sleep that melts our hearts and makes us long to sleep like a baby.

But that doesn't last forever. Once an infant adjusts to the world, one of the first lessons he must master is that of how to fall asleep and stay asleep. Cycles of going to sleep and staying asleep embed patterns in a child's mind and body for future habits. It will take some work to teach a growing baby, infant, and child to learn to sleep like a baby.

Why is it so important for a baby to develop healthy sleep behaviors?

- ∞ A well-rested child will be healthier, more engaged in relationships, and better able to learn.
- ∞ Well rested parents enjoy a better marriage and make better parents.
- ∞ The health of the whole family benefits from a baby who learns to sleep well.

Philosophies on sharing a family bed, sleep position-
ing, and soothing vary about as much and as often as an
expectant mom's appetite. Parents-to-be need to educate themselves from reliable sources that may include:
a trusted pediatrician, an older friend, or a wise relative.
Both parents need to rest if they are to face the challenges of family life together, so teaching your babe to
slumber should be a high priority in the first year.

Your baby needs to sleep so you can sleep. Only
use a monitoring system if you're able to sleep. Don't
worry that you have to be watching your babe every
moment as he breathes softly; the Lord will watch
over you all. "He will not let your foot be moved; he
who keeps you will not slumber. Behold, he who keeps
Israel will neither slumber nor sleep," (Psalm 121:3-4).
Isn't it comforting to know you can sleep because God
never does?

Children need to know how to fall asleep on their
own, how to fall back to sleep when they wake, and how
to settle themselves when restless. For many children,
these are not natural skills, but learned skills. Plan ahead
for the habits you want to carry into your tike's childhood as you answer:

∞ Where will the baby sleep on a regular basis?
∞ How will we put the baby to bed consistently?
∞ What habits can we maintain so both of us are
  involved and neither is drained?
∞ What will prepare our child to have healthy pat-
  terns of rest as he grows up?

New parents can count on some sleepless nights and blurry-eyed mornings. There will be days you know you need rest to be the wife and mother you need to be, but you'll wonder if deep sleep will ever return. It will. But while you're getting there, establish patterns for your little one that will teach her to have sweet sleep in her future.

Children are blessed when they know how to sleep like a baby, even when they're no longer babies.

Words to grow your heart

"It is good to give thanks to the LORD, to sing praises to your name, O Most High; to declare your steadfast love in the morning, and your faithfulness by night."
(Psalm 92: 1-2)

Thoughts to treasure in your heart or share with a friend

- ∞ What kind of bedtime routine are you and your husband expecting to work for you?
- ∞ What sleep needs do you have as parents and as a married couple?
- ∞ How can you prepare a restful sleep environment for your baby?
- ∞ How can you prepare as a couple for your bedroom to be peaceful?

First Sight

Until the moment of birth, your little one sees only darkness. What will be her first sight? The glaring lights of the delivery room? The back of a taxi? (Just kidding!) We hope it will be the smiling, loving faces of her parents. Do you remember your first sight? Probably not, but somewhere in your first years, you began to etch out memories, and your baby will too. What will be your baby's first memorable sight? Have you thought about what you want your baby's eyes to see?

As you plan a nursery and choose books, consider what you want to be your child's first memories. Children develop acceptance of and attachment to what we show them, to the things we express excitement about and the things that bring us joy. How can you prepare a child's heart to love what you value? Carefully choose the first images that enter your child's eye gate and lodge in his heart and mind.

Who or what do you want your child to love? Once you know what matters to your family, craft the atmosphere of your baby's room and home to provide their visual bank. Grandparents may not live nearby, but photos of family members develop early recognition and attachment for a baby's language and understanding. Images around children as they develop a cognitive framework for their surroundings prepare them to view, evaluate, and respond to their worlds. A child exposed to plants and animals at an early age will be more likely to appreciate and understand natural things, viewing them as a normal and basic part of the life they're comfortable with. Little ones who see illustrations of Bible stories develop familiarity and interest in who God is and in the spiritual, oral history they learn from their parents.

As parents our prayer may be that God would "Let the words of my mouth and the meditation of my heart be acceptable in your sight, O Lord, my rock and my redeemer," (Proverbs 19:14). Like a smart start with a baby's nutrition, healthy pre-reading skills, and wise habits with strangers, being thoughtful about building and protecting our babies' early thoughts prepares them to be comfortable with a clean heart.

What will you display on the walls of your baby's nursery or on the bookshelf in your home? Monkeys? Owls? Trains? They may start out with the hope of being a zookeeper, a "camper man," or an engineer, depending on how we adorn their world and steer their hearts. The mind and heart of a child is fertile ground for imprinting the images of first sight.

What will you say about the earliest images your baby takes in? Your words give your baby's world meaning. Make the most of the first times of recognition and interest, and keep repeating what's vital for them to know. From birth, the world competes for children's mental space, bombarding them with slick marketing, appealing colors, and enticing options. Parents spend a lifetime sorting through what to give their children access to, visually and otherwise. Start choosing wisely by thoughtfully providing their very first sights.

- ∞ "This is Grandma. Grandma loves you."
- ∞ "This is Noah. God took care of Noah."
- ∞ "This is Mommy and Daddy. Mommy loves Daddy."
- ∞ "This is a puppy. God made the puppy."
- ∞ "This is Jesus. Jesus loves children. Jesus loves you!"

Parents have the chance to show their child the world for the first time. Let's make the most of it.

Words to grow your heart

"Let the words of my mouth and the meditation of my heart be acceptable in your sight, O Lord, my rock and my redeemer." (Psalm 19:14)

Thoughts to treasure in your heart or share with a friend

- ∞ How will you feed your baby images to help her love the things you love?
- ∞ Consider your house now; what would people see that you value if they looked around with *first sight*?

Building the Future

A Bible for Baby

Every nursery needs books. Books smile at children as they grow aware of their world and curious about what they see. For the moment when a little one is ready to reach for a story, a book must stand ready to be grasped. Along with animals, stuffed toys, pictures of family, or sports gear, if you want children to love to read, they need to see books.

Fill a child's environment with what you want them to love. More than *Goodnight Moon* or *Are You My Mother?* or *I'll Love You Forever*, God's book is filled with treasures for childhood and beyond. Prepare your babe to be a child who wants to grasp a Bible by having one on hand, inviting your child to open it long before she's ready to turn a page.

A Bible for baby should be designed for young minds, with colorful illustrations to stimulate their eyes and mind to say, "These stories from God are for you." Bibles don't have to be tiny, but big enough for a toddler to hold and see and absorb. Stories may be paraphrased for developing understanding and vocabulary, but content should be truthful and accurate. Point to pictures that will help your small one learn the names of characters who will become as familiar as the Cat in the Hat. Have a Bible ready for you to share with Baby during quiet times or bedtimes or morning times.

"And these words that I command you today shall be on your heart. You shall teach them diligently to your children, and shall talk of them when you sit in your house, and when you walk by the way, and when you lie down, and when you rise." (Deuteronomy 6:6-7)

Most parents-to-be dream of planting a sport or a hobby on the heart of their child so they will share something sweet together. Plan to print God's stories on the heart of your little one, and you will share something sweeter than honey.

"The law of the LORD is perfect, reviving the soul; the testimony of the LORD is sure, making wise the simple; the precepts of the LORD are right, rejoicing the heart; the commandment of the LORD is pure, enlightening the eyes; the fear of the LORD is clean, enduring forever; the rules of the LORD are true, and righteous altogether. More to be desired are they than gold, even much fine gold; sweeter also than honey and drippings of the honeycomb." (Psalm 19:7-10)

So what's on Baby's bookshelf? This is the time to choose a copy of God's story that will nurture the very hearts of your children.

Words to grow your heart

"He established a testimony in Jacob and appointed a law in Israel, which he commanded our fathers to teach to their children, that the next generation might know them, the children yet unborn, and arise and tell them to their children, so that they should set their

hope in God and not forget the works of God, but
keep his commandments." (Psalm 78:5-7)

**Thoughts to treasure in your heart or share with a
friend**

- ∞ What books would make your top-ten list you want for your children?
- ∞ Do you have a favorite book you remember from your youngest years?
- ∞ Are God's stories in your child's library yet?
- ∞ If you don't have a Baby Bible yet, a visit to a Christian bookstore or browsing online would make a great part of a date night for two parents-to-be.

What's in a Name?

You could decide that your baby will be a "junior," or even "the third," or you could mimic a celebrity, a best friend, or a hero. Long ago, names were chosen to publically link a person to a family, to remember their circumstances of birth, or to foretell their destiny. The meaning of a name suggested the very essence of who the child would be. Even the announcement of the name of Jesus, Emmanuel, suggested He would be "God with us."

No one wants to burden a child with a name they'll have to live down for a lifetime or defend on the playground. Moms- and dads-to-be try out names and initials to avoid combinations leading to monograms like "D.U.D." or "R.A.T." And how about nicknames? As the forty weeks of pregnancy pass, parents try to think like a child in a classroom or a middle school peer, imagining how their baby's perfect name might be misconstrued.

What will your baby's name say about the essence of who you want her to be? After all, "A good name is to be chosen rather than great riches, and favor is better than silver or gold," (Proverbs 22:1). You will use this name to sing her to sleep, to confess your love to her, to call her in warning, to reprimand her in love, to pray for her, and to pronounce your belief in her. Your child's name will become precious to you.

Some moms-to-be have been dreaming of using a particular name for years, only to find their husbands never had the same vision. Couples come together to list possible winners, to eliminate the less favored options, and to narrow down their choices. Relatives and friends usually weigh in, though parents-to-be dread finding out that their extended circle of friends and family doesn't applaud their choice. Occasionally a name stirs up bad memories of an ex-boyfriend or ex-girlfriend, a pet, or a strong-willed youngster. Popular names encourage some parents to jump on the bandwagon, while others want to come up with a one-of-a-kind unique moniker as a title for their child. How do you choose the perfect name?

To choose the perfect name for your perfect child, you need more than a book with lists of possibilities. You need answers to important questions.

- ∞ Every child is on his way to adulthood; what kind of person do you want your child to become?
- ∞ Names conjure up connections; what qualities do you want to convey in the name you choose?
- ∞ A name is a gift; what names would be a gift of love to your little one?
- ∞ A child represents two people as one; do you both love the name?

Part of the adventure of parenting is the discovery of who your child will become. You cannot know her personality, her choices, or her future. You may give him a name suited for a poet and painter, only to watch him give the name new meaning when he becomes a scientist and explorer.

God knows your child's future, but He gives parents the privilege of choosing their baby's name. It's better than giving them "great riches," and it sets them on the path of becoming a one-of-a-kind person whose name will be music to your ears.

Words to grow your heart

"But now thus says the LORD, he who created you, O Jacob, he who formed you, O Israel: 'Fear not, for I have redeemed you; I have called you by name, you are mine.'" (Isaiah 43:1)

Thoughts to treasure in your heart or share with a friend

- ∞ Do you know what your name means? Your husband's name?
- ∞ Is there a name you've been waiting to use for your child? What does it mean to you?
- ∞ What names are on the top of your list? What makes them meaningful to you?
- ∞ Would you pray that God will show you the best name for your baby?

For the Love of Reading

Our first child's feet pushed and poked beneath my maternity dress, drawing out squeals of delight and giggles from my brood of first grade students and their moms. Just a week before my delivery, children and parents gathered around the classroom rocking chair to give us a baby shower. I had to reach over my mountain of a belly to give out hugs of appreciation for the many gifts of my students' favorite books. They started our family library with stories they loved, many we had shared together. Few gifts last as long as the love of reading.

No child is born into the world with a love of reading, but everyone is born to learn. Parents have the privilege and challenge of breathing life into a child's desire to learn.

At first, a book may be loved simply for the way the cardboard feels against teething gums, for the colors it adds to a nursery décor, or for the cuddling that comes when it's brought down from the shelf. To open a book with our little ones is to open ourselves and so much more.

A newborn baby sees best from about twelve inches away, which is just the right distance when you cradle her and hold a book in front of the two of you. High contrast images like those in black and white patterns catch their attention. As they grow older, books that invite physical engagement appeal to a child's developing small muscles. Lifting flaps and feeling a variety of textures rewards the attempts of little fingers to practice growing dexterity. Simple text and rhyming words complement vivid pictures and maximize a baby's short attention span, making the reading experience a pleasure. Little ones learn that story time means being encircled in love and security.

The most pleasant part of reading time comes when a baby learns that sharing books means it's time to be held in the warmth of a tender embrace. As a parent talks to listening little ones, they model sound and speech patterns that build vocabulary and language skills. Basic concepts of reading begin to take shape as a child becomes familiar with the action of turning pages, reading text in a left to right direction, identifying a name with a series of letters, matching words to pictures by pointing, and using tone and expression to add meaning. To open a book is to open the world to your curious babe at the prime time of her learning journey.

Do you want your child to have a lifelong love of learning and reading? Give him a love of books.

God loves the written word and even says He writes His very law on the hearts of His own. "But this is the covenant that I will make with the house of Israel after those days, declares the LORD: I will put my law within them, and I will write it on their hearts. And I will be their God, and they shall be my people," (Jeremiah 31:33). His word is a collection of stories and poetry and more. He keeps books of His own and wants us to know them.

Some children feel intimidated by the stories of the Bible, but when we teach our children to love reading, we prepare them to be willing to read God's book for themselves. Parents pave the way for children to open God's book of stories one day and discover His love for them.

You have the chance to write on your child's heart. If you want your child to enjoy being near to you and hearing the sound of your voice, make reading a part of life together from the first weeks. You will plant a love for relationship and for reading in their heart that will last for their lifetime.

Words to grow your heart

"You have kept count of my tossings; put my tears in your bottle. Are they not in your book? Then my enemies will turn back in the day when I call. This I know, that God is for me." (Psalm 56:8-9)

"Now there are also many other things that Jesus did. Were every one of them to be written, I suppose that the world itself could not contain the books that would be written." (John 21:25)

Thoughts to treasure in your heart or share with a friend

- ∞ Did you have a favorite book as a child?
- ∞ What do you associate with reading?
- ∞ What do you want your child to feel about books?
- ∞ If you haven't started a library for your child yet, now is a great time! Are there books you want your child to read and love?

First Things First

Her dark curls were disheveled around her face, and under her long eyelashes a storm brewed behind her eyes. Slightly plump cheeks puffed out in stubborn thought, and her arms crossed over her chest in determined rebellion. She hated the items her mama had put on her plate, and it was just a matter of moments before she began her assault to get her way. Uncomfortable onlookers braced for the fit, as the mom awkwardly explained how the attitude all began earlier that day.

She was wrong. The attitude began when her beautiful girl was just an angelic infant.

A well behaved child grows out of a well-trained infant.

Most healthy children will throw a fit at least once. It's part of testing their boundaries, trying out their independence, and seeing if their parents mean what they say. But have you been with children whose regular behavior includes tantrums, angry words, physically acting out, and rebellion? No one has to teach a child how to want their own way; after all, "for all have sinned and fall short of the glory of God," (Romans 3:23). In addition to their tiny fingers, baby smell, peach fuzz hair, and perfect lips, your babe is born with a sinful disposition.

The best time to teach children to behave well is when they're forming their view of themselves, you, and their world. Children feel most secure when environments include clearly defined, consistent boundaries, and they will act out in search of finding the boundaries and reinforcing them. To be firm and consistent is to demonstrate love.

Before she can sit up or crawl, a baby will test her power over you. It's a great power, so be prepared to snap out of your haze of adoration and do what's best for the training of your child.

∞ How long does he need to cry to be picked up?
∞ If he smiles how will you respond?
∞ When he spits out his cereal, will you stop feeding?
∞ Will you pick up his pacifier when he drops it?

Motherhood is meant to be enjoyed, so don't fear that you need to open *Baby Bootcamp*. However, consider now what kind of a child you will enjoy, and make small, daily decisions that will train your infant to become that kind of child. Think about the kind of behavior others will enjoy in your child, and shape your expectations to train your child to behave in that way. If you want to enjoy your child as she grows up, you must shape her will while it's still soft and pliable in the tender, loving, firm hands of a mother.

∞ Your child needs to know she is loved.
∞ Your child needs to know love sets boundaries.
∞ Your child needs to know *no* means *no*.
∞ Your child needs to know obedience brings joy.
∞ Your child needs to know rebellion brings sadness or pain.
∞ Your child needs to know her parents are her authority.

How will you know when to give in or when to hold your ground? Sweet mama, God has not left you alone in this all important question. He has given you His word to grant you wisdom (James 1:5), His Spirit to give you discernment (John 16:13), and mentors to filter the challenges of everyday mothering (Titus 2:3-5). Not only will He place a baby in your arms, but He will place intuition in your heart and mind that will enable you to make the decisions of ones called "mother."

When an infant learns that loving parents set

boundaries for her protection and good, she will grow to be a child who honors adults, relates to the idea of a loving Heavenly Father, and behaves in a pleasant way that others enjoy being around. Decide now what kind of a child you want to parent years from now, and train your baby to grow that way.

Words to grow your heart

> "If any of you lacks wisdom, let him ask God, who gives generously to all without reproach, and it will be given him." (James 1:5)

> "Discipline your son, and he will give you rest; he will give delight to your heart." (Proverbs 29:17)

Thoughts to treasure in your heart or share with a friend

∞ What behaviors do you think make a child enjoyable to be around?

∞ Do you know of children who model the kind of behavior you hope your baby will learn?

∞ What could you ask that mother, so that you discover some of her secrets?

∞ Finish this sentence, "Lord, I need the wisdom to know . . ."

School Daze

In modern times, there's just more. More for kids to learn. More children in classrooms. More for parents to worry about in traditional settings. More expectations for children to achieve. More curriculum to choose from. More options for how to educate your children. All the choices may leave new moms and dads feeling like they're caught in a school daze long before it's time to register or take that first-day-of-school photo.

Babies have barely begun to scoot and pull up on coffee tables when mommy friends at the park or church start to ask about pre-school and schooling plans. Suddenly, everyone is convinced her child is advanced, and everyone wants to figure out and share the *right way* to educate a child. Even before board books make way for paper copies of Dr. Seuss, some new parents have signed their kids up on waiting lists for preferred schools or have begun to collect materials they feel sure will put their babe on the genius track.

Parents-to-be know the familiar words of Psalm 139 and smile at the wonder of God watching over their unformed child in utero. "Your eyes saw my unformed substance," we read, "in your book were written, every one of them, the days that were formed for me, when as yet there was none of them," (Psalm 139:16). God has even greater plans than ours for every one of the days formed for our child. Our efforts will not take God's plan to a higher level or achievement, though we will have the pleasure of being part of His grand design for our precious one's potential.

Without being caught up in the current of rushing ahead into school days, consider what matters most to you as a family when making decisions about the style, timing, and setting for the education of your child.

For now, shut out the voices around you advocating public school, Christian school, home school, co-op school, boarding school, or virtual school. While you are still the primary teacher and trainer of your little charge, ask God for wisdom and help to consider what works best for your child and your family.

Every child is unique. Therefore, one type of schooling approach is not best for all children. Like diapers for newborns, one size does not really fit all. God directs parents to make the best decision for the child God has given them to raise. Each family has their own set of values, their own schedules, their own ministry goals, their own resources, and their own opportunities. One cannot judge the decisions of another. Families need to consider:

∞ What options are available to you?
∞ What are the needs of your particular child? Academic? Emotional? Social? Spiritual?
∞ What goals do you have for educating your child?
∞ What resources do you have for educating your child?
∞ How are you equipped as parents to participate in your child's learning?
∞ How do you both feel about the decision?

Parents need to be unified around the schooling decision. The academic piece of raising a child should not separate a couple or cause strife. It's not always easy to face the realities of your child's needs, your available resources, your own limitations, and your circumstances. You are on the same team when it comes to wanting what's best for your child's growth and development.

Parents will face changes in their family circumstances and in their children. As transitions arise, families may need to take new approaches to schooling. Each change brings teachable moments for moms and dads to do the most valuable teaching of all: trust in God and follow Him in all of life's lessons.

Words to grow your heart

"Train up a child in the way he should go; even when he is old he will not depart from it." (Proverbs 22:6)

Thoughts to treasure in your heart or share with a friend

∞ Describe your own experience in school. How were you educated?
∞ Do either of you have any prejudices or stereotypes about a particular style of schooling?
∞ What do you think matters most to your family in educating your children?
∞ Ask God to give you insights into your child's learning needs, your options, and your resources in the coming years.

THE NEW NORMAL

Managing Motherhood

Know Your Family Album

What will you give your baby from your own childhood? A silver spoon? A frayed teddy bear? The secret family pancake recipe? Your baby will be blessed if you sift through your childhood while preparing for his.

When moving into the new territory of mommy-hood, it helps to know where you came from. Once you have a pink stripe and a due date, all your thoughts may turn to the family you're growing, but pausing to look back helps you move forward.

How do children and adults relate to each other? What speaks comfort to you? How do you communicate? What atmosphere do you want in your home? How do you expect to discipline? What is the balance of work and play? Understanding how your family of origin shaped you from womb to woman reveals what influenced your earliest ideas of family life.

Since we are all born flawed, no one has a perfect heritage. For some moms-to-be, a careful look into their own family albums reveals a healthy, happy start nurtured into a thriving childhood. For others, looking back proves painful and uncovers questions to be answered and wounds to be healed. Every new mom benefits from understanding her own background, if she approaches it with an honest heart seeking to learn.

Your first steps influence your mothering, but they don't determine your pathway for parenting. Though she understands her own beginnings, a woman's legacy is her own to etch and leave for her child. If reflection on your history exposes a life you would not want to duplicate, be encouraged—the Heavenly Father makes the broken whole and the old new. Each new mom has the chance to be a *new* mom.

Even if a woman's roots include conflict, rest assured, "where sin increased, grace abounded all the more," (Romans 5:20b). Each of us can ask God to help us sift out a family heirloom to bring forward into our own mothering. Did your parents work hard? Did they value honesty? Did they love you? Did they encourage you? Did they show generosity? Did they persevere? Search through the attic of your heritage and find treasures to bring into your life as a mother.

Every new mother wants to be the perfect mother; every mother fails. Perfection is not a stage to be reached in your forty weeks of pregnancy or in your lifetime of mothering. Like our moms before us, we will wrestle with who we want to be and who we are. By God's grace we will parent our children the best way we can, and we will forge a new legacy to leave behind. Your tattered teddy bear and family pancakes will add to the sweet heritage you prepare for your little one. The pages of your family album are just beginning to be filled.

Someday a grown person will want to understand where they came from; give them a history full of truth and beauty and love to discover.

Words to grow your heart

"Know therefore that the Lord your God is God, the faithful God who keeps covenant and steadfast love with those who love him and keep his commandments, to a thousand generations." (Deuteronomy 7:9)

Thoughts to treasure in your heart or share with a friend

- ∞ What treasures do you bring from your family of origin that you want to continue?
- ∞ Are there new patterns you hope to set that will be different from your own experience?
- ∞ What words would you want your child to use to describe the legacy you leave to them someday?

Yielding Zone

When your babe has started to pull up and toddle, you will have started gently walking her through the lesson of what it is to let go. Let go of a nighttime feeding. Months later (or years?), let go of a pacifier. Let go of diapers. Let go of sleeping with an angel-soft, satin-edged blanky.

Growing up demands walking the path of letting go.

Our small ones are not the only ones learning to let go. Moms-to-be join throngs of women before them who have released their grips on favorite habits out of necessity and mommy-love. Long, hot showers. Lazy Saturday mornings in bed. Spreading out accessories in the bathroom and taking uncounted time to get ready for the day. Growing out long, well-shaped nails painted in unsmeared, glossy brights.

But then a pudgy hand reaches up to grasp a hand full of well-groomed strands of hair. As eye-hand coordination develops, a babe cannot resist wrapping eager fingers around a favorite dangling earring and giving a tug towards a curious mouth. The unfolding life of a child demands that a mother learn to yield.

Just because we love our little explorers does not mean we will not grieve the necessary yielding as we transition into a new kind of woman, a mother. Like a child crying for a night feeding or longing for a hit from a binky, our hearts may thirst for the comfort of our pre-babe habits. Those indulgences may not be gone forever, but they may require we set them aside for a season.

As a child grows up to independence, a mother grows up in godliness. A mommy learns not to do things out of self-centeredness, but to act in humility, to count other people as more important than herself (Philippians 2:3) on a whole new level. There is no room for selfishness in the nursery of a well-loved child.

The degree of unselfishness learned in the classroom of marriage intensifies when a baby is added to the mix.

While new daddies experience the joy of new baby love, adding a swing to the living room or turning the man cave into a playroom may stretch even the most attentive dad. Fathers are on their own learning curves of yielding as they practice willingness to warm bottles or change diapers before making their own coffee in the morning. When he makes an advance on his wife for an intimate conquest, a new dad may grieve the disappointment when he is met by a breastfeeding mommy tired of being touched or being kept awake in the night. Daddy learns to yield too.

A woman grows in godliness when she learns to yield herself to someone whose needs are more important than her own. Like her little one crying over lost comforts, a mom may yearn for the luxurious days of having her way. What our babes do not know is that by letting go of once-sweet habits, they open their hands and hearts to new and wonderful things. The same holds true for the mommy who toddles along her own path of yielding.

Maybe having a baby or adding a child to life is more about us becoming holy than about making us happy. As we let go of temporary soothers and release our grips on what we think we need, better and more enduring discoveries take the place of old things. New joys. New comforts. Rewards for moms who learn to yield.

Words to grow your heart

"Let each of you look not only to his own interests, but also to the interests of others. Have this mind among yourselves, which is yours in Christ Jesus, who, though he was in the form of God, did not count equality with God a thing to be grasped, but made himself nothing, taking the form of a servant, being born in the likeness of men." (Philippians 2:4-7)

Thoughts to treasure in your heart or share with a friend

- ∞ What habit makes you cringe when you think of setting it aside?
- ∞ How do you think baby's daddy will respond to the need to yield his habits?
- ∞ What do you think a family looks like when a mommy does not yield her habits?
- ∞ What do you think yielding your habits will do for your family life?
- ∞ How can you include some comfort times for yourself when a baby is in your life?

Watching the Clock

What are you supposed to do all day when you are home with a baby? Time never crept by when meetings, reports, appointments, breaks, and quitting time marked the hours. During the first days baby arrives at home, it may fill the time to practice feeding, go to appointments, and receive visitors, but what about when the routines become routine? What then?

How does a mom use her day when she is home alone with just her babe to pass the time? Without some thoughtful plans and friendly accountability, a new mom may find herself making excuses for living every day in sweatpants and talking about daytime TV hosts like they're her new BFF. Moving from a career to a nursing bra may sound romantic, but when the newness wears off and turns into everyday life, women may experience new labor pains. This radical change requires a shift in our thinking and acquisition of new skills.

There was a time when a day at home meant a vacation day or sick day. When a new mom stays home for maternity leave temporarily or long term, she is no longer off for the day or home to rest. Instead of waking up to a free day, she wakes up to redeem her time. She has the opportunity to plan her work, care for her home, and nurture her family, so she will reap a harvest. She still considers priorities and efficiency, but she does it from home. No day is the same, and each day is unpredictable. "Whatever you do, work heartily, as for the Lord and not for men . . . You are serving the Lord Christ," (Colossians 3:23-24).

A new mom admitted her surprise at feeling trapped inside her home, not sure how to spend her days, trying to conjure up ideas to get out. Strangely, though, the equally new dad admitted how overwhelmed he felt; each day he came home to an exhausted wife, a restless child, a messy house, and pleas for eating out. Instead of managing the day to take care of her home, prepare a meal, interact with her baby, and feed her spirit, the new mom just endured and tried to stay occupied until daddy arrived to hear her cries and provide an emergency evacuation. He dreaded coming home. Both knew their jaundiced start needed some light to bring it to good health. Mom had to think of her days in a new way.

Any mommy can survive a day at home, but an excellent mommy thrives in her day at home. Do you have an occasional survival day? Or do you have an occasional thriving day? What kind of mommy do you want to be?

It takes a whole new set of skills to stay home well. A lot of women give up before they learn how to spend a day at home successfully. Like any career, we need to seek training, practice what we learn, evaluate our progress, and stay at it on the good days and the bad. There is a learning curve for planning meals, managing household supplies, self-directing a schedule, and knowing a child's needs. It takes proficiency and effort to create an atmosphere of warmth and love. Our own expectations challenge us when we are constantly required to be flexible, selfless, and patient. Wise moms connect with other moms in seasons beyond their own and in their own to find the practical help and support needed to transition to a new way of spending time.

Questions to consider when planning your day:

∞ Have you met with the Lord to feed and guide your spirit and mind?
∞ Is your house clean and comfortable to provide a peaceful atmosphere?
∞ How have you interacted with your child in mean-

ingful, stimulating ways?

∞ What friendships are you investing in by spending time together?

∞ How have you prepared your home and self for your husband?

Staying home with a child is new territory for most women. Though you have longed for the privilege, that does not make it easy. But nothing worthwhile comes easy.

If you plan to accomplish nothing, you will. Instead of approaching these home days as less important than your career days, consider them as highly valued, because "You are serving the Lord Christ" in your home. For however many days you have at home, make the most of them. Shift your thinking and develop your skills for this new and highly cherished task of being a mom in her home. You do not have time to watch the clock.

Words to grow your heart

". . . train the young women to love their husbands and children, to be self-controlled, pure, working at home, kind, and submissive to their own husbands, that the word of God may not be reviled." (Titus 2:4-5)

Thoughts to treasure in your heart or share with a friend

∞ What do you miss from your pre-baby days? Share this with a friend.

∞ Is there some part of caring for your home that is hard for you or makes you turn green?

∞ Who is in your life from the next season to help you know how to manage baby days?

∞ Who is in your life from your same season to push her stroller beside you?

∞ Many women use planners or schedules in their career fields. What similar mommy tool can you try to direct your day?

∞ In the morning, ask God to show you how to redeem each day, and every now and then, give yourself a day off!

To Work or Not to Work

Before bringing babies into their lives, most women work outside the home to help build a strong financial cradle for the family. But when a child joins the mix, bringing with it needs and demands and decisions, couples find themselves dealing with the very personal question of whether or not to work?

No one else knows your family's needs like you do, and no one else can claim your family's blessings for you. Many well-meaning friends and family members will weigh in on the plans for mom's post-baby employment, but ultimately the decision falls to mommy and daddy. Wherever you land in your plans, the question of work brings with it unavoidable transitions. New parents discover that best doesn't always mean easy, and it usually means hard.

Ask yourself a lot of questions: If you stay home, how will you manage financially? Will you miss your profession? Will you feel fulfilled? What will your days look like? Will daycare hurt your child?

While you cannot know the answers to all of these questions and more, you can be confident about some things:

∞ You have work. It is work to raise a child and care for him physically, emotionally, mentally, and spiritually.

∞ You cannot do it all. Many moms have tried, but no one can do it all without accepting some losses.

∞ You have to make choices. You have to choose what you and your husband are willing to count as losses. Think about the priorities you share and make decisions based on those.

∞ You have others to consider. If you are married, you have a spouse to consider, and you need to share one heart in this matter. Like all of your decisions now, your course will impact your child.

∞ You have a one-of-a-kind identity. You are a mom and so much more.

∞ You have an ideal and a reality. Each mom has to reconcile where her dreams end and her necessities begin.

∞ You have truth to guide you. God promises us wisdom and all we need for life in His word. There is no need to flounder without helpful principles.

∞ You have God to provide for you. If you choose to live on a single income or a limited income, God is still the provider of all you need. He knows your needs.

∞ You have a lifetime ahead of you. Aim now for your future target. What kind of child and marriage and family do you desire? Your choices now will point you there.

∞ You have a guarantee. We have the freedom to decide what we sow, but we will reap what we sow.

A mother's heart longs and waits for her child, but most women have also invested time and energy and resources in developing a professional life. If opinions press in from others in baby's life, remember to ask, "For am I now seeking the approval of man, or of God? Or am I trying to please man? If I were still trying to please man, I would not be a servant of Christ," (Galatians 1:10). Someone will not be happy with the decision your family makes, but ultimately, God is at the top of a mom's corporate ladder.

Despite our joy at becoming moms, it is not easy to make career transitions. Whether women decide to be a 100% stay-at-home mom, a part-time employee, or a full-time employee, mothering upends work life. The combination of career and mothering may result in grief, guilt, tears, or conflict. Be patient with yourself and your husband as you communicate about the changes you experience while figuring out the new work of motherhood.

Words to grow your heart

"Do not be deceived: God is not mocked, for whatever one sows, that will he also reap." (Galatians 6:7)

Thoughts to treasure in your heart or share with a friend

∞ How do you feel about your pre-baby profession?
∞ What does your husband need and desire from you in the motherhood-work transition?
∞ Do you have strong feelings about any particular option?
∞ Have you experienced input from others around you?
∞ Ask God to show you and your husband what He desires for your family and to provide for you as you follow Him through the work-life changes that parenting brings.

Calling the Shots

"Mrs. Sanders, you will never stop needing to worry." The cold words of the pediatric neurologist settled on my mind and heart like a falling tree. Never? How could that be, since we had been so careful to read all we could, follow all the doctor's orders, and work so hard in the first five months of our infant girl's life? As I snapped the baby carrier into the car and turned up the heat, grief overwhelmed me as I realized I had never really been in control at all and never would be.

Every new parent imagines they can be in careful control of everything that enters their babies' lives. Our hearts want only what's good and right and healthy and best. We read all we can before the first vaccinations, ask a new-parent-load of questions, and then brace ourselves for the pain, hoping we did what's best. But we can't know it all or control it all.

When and if those first shots come, the children of our hearts cry out in shock and dismay that we allowed pain to take over, but they nuzzle into our shoulder with confident trust we are still the safest place of all.

We may be tempted to direct every detail of our pregnancy plans and birthing plans and parenting plans, as if we are in total control of seeing every need and desire met. Everything will be perfect if we plan it that way, right? But no child's life is perfect, just like no pregnancy is perfect and no parent is perfect. Imperfections and problems are not listed on a registry, because no one would choose them.

Who is the safest place of all, the One who calls the shots?

After years of following Jesus and feeling safe with Him, his disciples realized they had no control of their circumstances. Their Lord had been arrested and crucified. Many of His followers scattered. The Roman government hated anyone who identified with Him. They had all left their careers and taken on new ways of life.

They did not know they had a bright and purposeful future ahead of them, so when Jesus approached, He first told them, "Do not be afraid," (Matt. 28:10b). Since He could see what the days ahead would bring, He knew they had to understand two things that would give them peace.

> "And Jesus came and said to them, 'All authority in heaven and on earth has been given to me,'"
> (Matthew 28:18).

> "And behold, I am with you always, to the end of the age," (Matthew 28:20b).

Nothing will happen in our lives as parents or in the lives of our children that God has not allowed. His authority is based on who He is, and His character is completely just and good. While we want to control each event in the story of our babies' lives, God knows your little one's future and can work for her best. If it happens in heaven or on earth, He's got it covered.

There will never be a time when our children are out of God's sight or apart from His presence. While we cannot be present to watch over every bite taken, every new skill attempted, all people encountered, or each decision made, the Heavenly Father will be with us and with our little loves as they grow from babe to kid to teen to adult.

New moms would love to call the shots from day one in the lives of their children, but we need not fear when we know God oversees it all and He will always be there.

Words to grow your heart

> "When I am afraid, I put my trust in you. In God, whose word I praise, in God I trust; I shall not be afraid. What can flesh do to me?" (Psalm 56:3-4)

"Peace I leave with you; my peace I give to you. Not as the world gives do I give to you. Let not your hearts be troubled, neither let them be afraid." (John 14:27)

". . . for God gave us a spirit not of fear but of power and love and self-control." (2 Timothy 1:7)

Thoughts to treasure in your heart or share with a friend

∞ How does it make you feel to think you are not in control of your baby's life?
∞ What do you think a mom can do to balance trust with diligence to care for her babe?
∞ What areas of raising a child cause you to feel fearful? Ask God to give you peace there.

Habits You Can Live With

Small Parts Warning

Before she starts changing diapers, a new mom learns to watch for warning stickers to alert her that small parts pose a choking hazard. Because of the potential for danger, parents outlaw such toys or gadgets from a baby's environment. Some may choose to allow risky items in their households, but only with strict guidelines about storing them out of reach and limiting their use. But what about small items without warning labels, items with the potential to suffocate the heart of your child and the relationship newly born between you?

Today many parents welcome items into their daily lives without recognizing the danger they invite. Technology has gradually emerged in day to day, hour-by-hour life like a first tooth slowly breaking through a gum line. It's been pressing in without being noticed, until one day it appears, ready to bite us. Without even noticing the effect until the damage is felt, parents may miss out on so much of life with their babes, just because of their failure to tame the tech in their lives. Technical devices deserve a warning sticker in a new baby's home.

Communication changes have overflowed into our households and personal lives. Handy and hand-held, devices are so convenient that many people find they have developed a dependence on their online connections and access to information. Moms may respond to a fear that they are missing out on knowing something important while they are at home with their babies. Like a baby sucks a thumb just because it's there or cries for a pacifier because she is so accustomed to the stimulation, adults may check for an update, a message, or a piece of information as naturally as breathing. But like that wonderful, satisfying, delicious, addictive thumb on your babe's pudgy hand, sucking without thinking can lead to a raw, sore mess and distorted growth costing a lot to correct.

It takes self-control to put some good things into their rightful place in our lives. We model this for our children when we practice self-control before them in areas as basic as our own gadget use. Experienced mothers are instructed to teach new moms "to be self-controlled . . . that the Word of God may not be reviled," (Titus 2:3b-5). When we tame the tech in our lives, we display the word of God in our families.

Whether a little one finds comfort in a pacifier or a grownup finds comfort in staying up and involved in social media, a parent risks a constant pull away from her child at a time that only comes once. If tech is not tamed, new moms may grow into mommies who are unavailable, unfocused, and unobservant.

The only way an infant has to ask for mom's attention is to act out, to cry, and to fuss. Babies who learn to recapture their mother's attention negatively while in the car seat or highchair are more likely to grow into children and teenagers who act out in negative ways to try and get their parents' attention.

We would not ignore the small-parts warning on a toy we offer to our child or keep out in the open on the coffee table. Tech deserves a relationship warning, but it is here to stay in the lives of moms and dads and their children. Discuss and agree on boundaries for times when you will put limits on responding to the beeps, vibrations, and ringtones. Like you would with any threatening object, put tech away where it is not tempting or easily accessible. Instead of letting technology run your family life, decide together where and how you will allow those small parts to be part of your day to day life together.

Words to grow your heart

"But the fruit of the Spirit is love, joy, peace, patience, kindness, goodness, faithfulness, gentleness, self-control; against such things there is no law." (Galatians 5:22-23)

"A man without self-control is like a city broken into and left without walls." (Proverbs 25:28)

Thoughts to treasure in your heart or share with a friend

∞ What technical devices are part of your daily lives as a couple?

∞ Do gadgets come between you now in your marriage? What boundaries do you have?

∞ Would it help you to make a warning label and put it on your most frequently used device as a reminder?

Planning Your Day

We arrived at the festival just as the crowd was growing excited. My husband moved away from us to find a good position for taking pictures, leaving me holding the hands of our two young children. Like a living thing, the crowd seemed to draw us in, sucking at the kids as I tightened my grip. Sensing its growing power, I pulled my two treasures close and charged out of the mass of people as only a frightened mother can, shocked at how quickly we were being swept away by the chaos. Finding a safe place outside of the commotion, we regrouped and made a plan, unwilling to let our family be overtaken.

When a woman steps into the shoes of motherhood, she may feel swept up in the chaos of things she did not expect to be so powerful. Keeping a grip on productive days she can be proud of may prove harder than she imagined. Evening may find her wondering where the day went, what she did, and how she can make tomorrow different. The life of a mommy brings new ways to spend your days.

Like entering any new field, a learning curve awaits. While tutorials, classes, books, mentors, and reading may be offered to those taking on new careers, moms might find the need for similar resources to learn how to master the skills of *mommy days*. As we do in tackling other responsibilities, fresh tools of the trade may be needed like menu planners, calendar tools, and resources. How do you plan your days successfully when you're a mom? After all, an excellent mother is one who, "looks well to the ways of her household and does not eat the bread of idleness," (Proverbs 31:27).

The mom who approaches her new challenge with a learner's perspective will already find herself better equipped to resist being swept away by the things baby adds to daily life: feeding, changing, sleeping, feeding, bathing, burping, feeding, laundry. Each seems innocent when taken alone, but as a crowd, there's a power in the commotion they create.

A productive new mommy begins planning her day with prayer, even if it's only a short, sleepy-eyed plea for the Lord to guide her day and help her think clearly about her priorities. Ask God for the strength and wisdom and joy you need to resist being swept away by the day and, instead, to walk it out with His goals in mind. Without prayer, we leave out the divine direction we so desperately need.

A productive new mommy begins by thinking carefully about her plans for the day. God has given us wisdom to consider how we will care for our homes, our husbands, our children, and ourselves. Reflect on the most pressing needs and what speaks love to each one. Think about how to meet your own needs so you are able to be the wife and mother you want to be.

A productive new mommy begins by looking ahead to the end of the day. What do you want the outcome of the day to be? What would make it a successful day for you? It may change from day to day. To enjoy this new life as a mother, do you need to have dinner ready? Have spent some time in awe of your baby's eyes? A peaceful heart? Some energy for your husband? What is your goal today?

A woman has the privilege of being commissioned to nurture her family. She also has twenty-four limited hours each day to care for herself and for her loved ones. We need to plan and spend our hours and energy well.

Give yourself grace to practice the skills of planning mommy days. There probably will not be the same accountability as with many careers where regular evaluations, observations, HR reports, and productivity studies keep us striving to do well. No one will ask how you are doing, how you are growing, and what you produced. Only God and your husband and your little one will see the way you spend your days. Challenge yourself to keep learning and growing in how you are planning each day, for the good of your baby, your family, and yourself.

Words to grow your heart

"The plans of the heart belong to man, but the answer of the tongue is from the Lord. All the ways of a man are pure in his own eyes, but the Lord weighs the spirit. Commit your work to the Lord, and your plans will be established." (Proverbs 16:1-3)

"The heart of a man plans his way, but the Lord establishes his steps." (Proverbs 16:9)

Thoughts to treasure in your heart or share with a friend

∞ What tools do you use now that help you plan your days?
∞ What do you think a typical successful day looks like?
∞ What can you do now to start each day so you plan for success and productivity?

Finding a Mentor

Early that day I determined to feed our little ones well, teach them creatively, and love them attentively. My husband was working late, and I finished cleaning up the toys for more times than I could count. By the afternoon, our toddler was busy and our baby was sleeping. I was wearing thin when I heard the knock. Through the curtain I saw a woman old enough to be my mom, smiling and waving back at me. Opening the door, she greeted me warmly, looked in my eyes, and asked slowly,

"How are you doing? Are you doing okay?"

Women who have walked the motherhood road know the look of a mommy wearing thin. She had seen signs written on my eyes the day before, so she stopped in to check on me. Without my family members nearby, an interested older lady in my life was a gift. More than that, she was a mentor.

Why do you need a mentor?

Many new moms enter parenthood without a close or supportive relative in their daily lives, yet there is so much to learn. While friends of our same age and stage may commiserate as companions on the growing family journey, they lack the kind of wisdom and experience born from walking ahead and looking back. Women are not meant to walk alone into motherhood. Every mommy needs a mentor.

Where do you find a mentor?

Not every new or expectant mom has a mentor knock on her door and invite herself in, but they can be found. Look wherever you find loving families who nurture and train up their children. A church, women's group, neighborhood, or workplace may be the place; look wherever caring women do daily life. If "Her children rise up and call her blessed," (Proverbs 31:28a), she can walk alongside a younger woman on the journey. Ask God to show you a woman who has a mother's heart to mentor.

Who is a mentor?

A mentor is a woman who knows grace. She did not mother with perfection, but she understands a woman needs to grow into her new nurturing role. If you look for a flawless lady, you will not find her, but you can find someone whose first-hand experience with God's grace in her life equips her to share it with another woman.

A mentor is a woman who knows motherhood. She faced hardships and disappointments of her own, but she turned to God and learned from the challenges. Look for children who bless their mom, and then spend some time with that mother. With His truth engraved on her heart, she will guide you.

How will she help you?

A mom's heart learns the sweetness of nurturing others. She will embrace, encourage, and exhort you.

- ∞ She will embrace you, accepting your strengths and weaknesses, your failures and your victories. She understands, and she will embrace the mother you are.
- ∞ She will encourage you, cheering you on in stressful times and inspiring you to keep going. She walked the mother road beyond you, and she knows the rewards if you do not give up.
- ∞ She will exhort you. At a time in your life when you need guidance and wisdom, she will share hard-won lessons and point you to truths for your problems.

As your mentor walks alongside you, she will pray for you with the insight and love of a fellow mother. She knows how much better we mother when we do not try to do it alone, so she will cheer you on the motherhood road.

It may seem far away and even impossible now, but

someday your grown children will call you blessed, and you will recognize the fatigue written in the eyes of a younger mom. Go knock on her door and invite yourself into her life and ask her, "How are you doing?"

Words to grow your heart

"Two are better than one, because they have a good reward for their toil. For if they fall, one will lift up his fellow. But woe to him who is alone when he falls and has not another to lift him up!" (Ecclesiastes 4:9-10)

Thoughts to treasure in your heart or share with a friend

- ∞ Where are the potential mentors around you?
- ∞ What older or grown children do you know who bless their mom?
- ∞ You could invite a possible mentor to have coffee or go for a walk; ask about her journey as a mom, and share yours. Ask God to open the door for more regular informal or formal mentoring with this wise mom.

Mothers Need Others

The anticipation of a baby draws friends and family around an expectant mom. Showers and appointments bring loved ones together, while pictures of the growing baby bump and ultrasounds make the mom-to-be an overnight celebrity. Once the babe has arrived and well-wishes have been given, however, many new moms find themselves facing feelings of isolation.

Since their own lives have not undergone a major change, the officemates and girlfriends who watched the first thrusts of baby's foot from inside the womb may go on with their usual schedules and interests. A first time mom may feel alone in her unfamiliar world. New moms need other people.

Even though mothers need others, it may not be so easy to find companions whose schedules fit that of a mom with an infant. "A man of many companions may come to ruin, but there is a friend who sticks closer than a brother," (Proverbs 18:24). As former friendships take on new dimensions, a first time mama will long for a friend who is like a sister to her.

Limitations like location and transportation have the potential to add to the companionship challenge. Fatigue from the demands of a newborn may pose a temptation to just stay home, isolated from family and friends. With all of the novel needs she encounters in caring for her baby, a mom may convince herself it is too complicated or risky to take her little one out on her own. Since each day involves learning and experiment-ing, the thought of packing up a baby and his supplies may arouse a sense of anxiety or worry over the unpre-dictable nature of days out. It is not easy to get out when you are worn out.

If the obstacles to going out and reaching out remain, a new mom runs the risk of becoming depressed. In losing touch with others, she may suffer from a narrowing of her perspective, letting her own problems and doubts become bigger than they are. Time spent with other people has a way of providing a reality check and insight, shedding light on our troubles. Mothers need others.

Infants need others, too. While routine for a baby is like sunshine for a flower, little people in their first season grow healthier with the input of others. Varied stimulation of new voices, intonation, facial expressions, and personalities helps a baby learn to adapt to people besides her mother. Developing a comfort level with different people prepares a baby to suffer less separation anxiety later on and to respond with more ease socially. A baby who only knows how to feel secure in isolation will feel more stress when the time comes to interact with others, whether they are family, friends, or strangers. Children need others.

Despite the way it feels sometimes in the new baby world, there are others who need to get out too. Look in your community for other women just beginning the parenting journey and reach out to them through women's events, group gatherings, playdates, workshops, coffee dates, lunch invitations, walks, or phone calls. And when you need to go out, do not let the baby gear and the unexpected events of life with an infant discourage you or ruin your determination to be a healthy mom and babe.

Find those other mothers who need others and get out together. You will bless each other and your babies as you encourage one another to be companions on your new adventure of motherhood.

Words to grow your heart

"Iron sharpens iron, and one man sharpens another."
(Proverbs 27:17)

Thoughts to treasure in your heart or share with a friend

∞ What obstacle is most likely to keep you from getting out?
∞ What destinations, activities, or relationships motivate you to go out?
∞ Simplicity makes it easier to go out. How can you simplify your gear when you go out with baby?

Her Baby

The two baby-peers toddled around, exploring under the watchful eyes of their moms and extended families vacationing together. About the one with cherub cheeks and golden curls, comments were sprinkled on the mommy like glitter on a star; "She's so cute!" they all agreed. And while they cooed and cuddled, her baby-peer wandered curiously nearby, looking up in response to high pitched tones and happy voices meant for her birth friend; her mommy was silent.

Before they ever talked of ballet classes or school plays or prom dresses, the two little girls were being compared. Their mamas felt it too, though one felt downcast and the other felt proud.

Every new parent experiences the awe of their miraculous child, finding that imperfections add to their little one's uniqueness and individuality. Despite the fact God sees it that way too, a new mom soon feels pressure brought on by differences. It is easy to compare ourselves and our children to "her and her baby."

Observe any floor full of commando-crawling infants, and differences emerge. Developmental variations appear when babes roll side by side, one lifting its head high, another rolling into a sitting position, and another bursting out with the coveted, "Mama!" Instead of joy in the child of her prayers, a mother fights worry over what her child does not do or say. A sense of disappointment begs to find a home in her heart and sometimes threatens to create distance in the mother-child relationship if not dealt with head on.

Every honest mom battles comparison sometimes, because we all want the world to agree that our babies are the treasures we know them to be. The temptation to compare our children with others uncovers our own tendency to compare ourselves to other women. Baby differences remind us of our differences.

∞ Others have different advantages. Maybe they can stay at home full-time, send their kids to pre-school, buy adorable clothes first hand, or drive the latest minivan.

∞ Others have different circumstances. They were able to remodel their nursery, deliver naturally, breast feed, or get nighttime help from a baby-wise husband.

∞ Others are different as women. Her baby weight came off quickly; she gets a lot of sleep, uses the church nursery with ease, and didn't fight baby blues.

Others. Comparison is all about others, as if God withholds the best things from moms He loves less.

It is easier than ever to be tempted by comparison, since we see the lives of others presented through pictures and statements on social media. New moms do not even have to wait for a real-world playdate to see the differences in themselves, their children, and their families. Comparison closes in on new moms in private, as well as in public.

What has God given you? He designed your family uniquely, like no other. The contented mother says, "The lines have fallen for me in pleasant places; indeed, I have a beautiful inheritance," (Psalm 16:6).

Contentment answers comparison. Remember the satisfaction you felt when you looked in the eyes of your child for the first time? You celebrated her differences and found yourself speechless at the miracle God gave to you. Like the first creation, His design of your child is "very good."

Contentment is all about God.

"Keep your life free from the love of money, and be content with what you have, for he has said, 'I will never leave you nor forsake you,'" (Hebrews 13:5). Contentment brings freedom. Moms are meant to live free from wishing we had something else, that our lives were more like hers and less like the ones God gave us.

Her baby is just right for her, and your baby is just right for you. Content mothers do less comparing of deficits created by differences and more comparing of the blessings created by the God who made your little miracle. You are the mama God has chosen for your little one, and you are "very good."

Words to grow your heart

"Not that I am speaking of being in need, for I have learned in whatever situation I am to be content.
I know how to be brought low, and I know how to abound. In any and every circumstance, I have learned the secret of facing plenty and hunger, abundance and need. I can do all things through him who strengthens me." (Philippians 4:10-13)

Thoughts to treasure in your heart or share with a friend

∞ What do you love most about your babe, your husband, your family, and yourself?

∞ Are there differences in your family that make you unique?

∞ Can you thank God for drawing the lines of your life in "pleasant places"?

Acknowledgments

I consider myself blessed to have had my husband Jeff navigate the parenting journey with me. Becoming a father shook his expectations as much as becoming a mother shook mine, but he has been a hands-on dad from the first days in the NICU and in all of the adventures of raising two children together. Not only has he given me wings as a mom, but he has actively encouraged me to give birth to my love of writing and to pour myself into *Expectant*. He has lifted me up to minister to women around the world. I'm so grateful for his commitment to help me grow as a woman, a mom, and a writer. My family has been patient and supportive to allow me time to write, think, and create, even if it means a few more pizzas for dinner.

My own mom imprinted an understanding of mothering on my heart. She has lived out her own journey of motherhood before me, and I'm thankful God chose to write me into her story. Because of her love and nurturing in our lives, my heart became expectant for children of my own.

Teri Lynne Underwood and Sandra Peoples poured out gifts of input and insight as this book took shape. Fellow writers, moms, and dreamers, both generously shared their skills with me to breathe life into my ideas as they came together into a collection of devotions for moms.

Writers need friends who will be honest, but encouraging, and it's a bonus if they're willing to help edit at the last minute. Carol has ministered to my heart and in my manuscript, cheering me on and helping me grow. How grateful I am for the gift of her friendship to me.

My editor James Logan made me swallow my mama-pride! Who knew a *man* could add so much to a book for new and expectant *mothers*? James helped to bring the project full-term and deliver something I can share with joy. Jessica Kristie of Winter Goose Publishing created a publishing experience exceeding my hopes and expectations. I'm so grateful for Genny Heikka, who introduced me to The Hallway Project which brought *Expectant* to life.

The fellow mamas and bloggers of The MOM Initiative team qualify as a divine provision in my life. God clearly gathered us around our common love of His truth, nurturing the next generation, and mentoring moms to be all they can be in Christ. My sweet sisters add joy to the work of reaching out to moms, and they challenge and help me to offer God my best through speaking, writing, teaching, serving, and mentoring. Their confidence and partnership helped me find my way along the publishing journey. We really are better together.

About the Author

With the heart of a gentle mentor and inspirational teacher, Julie Sanders relays her passion to see people find God through writing truth for life online and Bible education for women in all walks of life. As a pastor's wife, Julie  travels internationally feeding a common need among people to know God's peace. While at home, she touches the lives of others through her internet home, *Come Have a Peace*. Julie calls the Southern United States her home, where she and her husband savor time with their two nearly-grown children.

Connect with Julie at juliesanders.org, where she offers peace for your days by sharing God's truth for the things of life, marriage, and parenting.

Find her on Twitter at *@JulieSanders_*, and join in the conversations about *Expectant* on Facebook, facebook.com/ComeHaveAPeace.

You can also find Julie writing with The MOM Initiative and The MOB Society teams, where moms are passionate about mentoring other moms. As you grow your family, she will help you grow your expectant heart on the journey of motherhood.